30-MINUTE MIDDLE EASTERN COOKBOOK

30-Minute
MIDDLE EASTERN
Cookbook

CLASSIC RECIPES MADE SIMPLE

Dorothy Calimeris

R
ROCKRIDGE
PRESS

First Rockridge Press trade paperback edition 2022

Rockridge Press and the Rockridge Press logo are trademarks or registered trademarks of Callisto Media Inc. and/or its affiliates in the United States and other countries and may not be used without written permission.

For general information on our other products and services, please contact our Customer Care Department within the United States at (866) 744-2665, or outside the United States at (510) 253-0500.

Paperback ISBN: 978-1-63807-050-4 | eBook ISBN: 978-1-63807-579-0

Manufactured in the United States of America

Interior and Cover Designer: Catherine San Juan
Art Producer: Maya Melenchuk
Editor: Anna Pulley
Production Editor: Matthew Burnett
Production Manager: David Zapanta

Photography © Elysa Weitala, cover; Shutterstock, pp. ii-iii, x, 84, 106, 126; iStock, pp. vi, vii, 116; J.R. Photography/Stocksy, p. vii; StockFood/ Lilia Jankowska, p. 18; Nuria Seguí/Stocksy, p. 36; StockFood/ Gräfe & Unzer Verlag/Schardt, Wolfgang, p. 48; StockFood/für ZS Verlag, p. 64. Food styling by Victoria Woollard, cover.

Author photography courtesy of Anne Kim

Cover recipe: Shawarma-Spiced Chicken, p. 69

10 9 8 7 6 5 4 3 2 1

I dedicate this book
to all the chefs and cooks
in the world who use food
to bring us together and
to share our cultures
and experiences.

Za'atar,
page 120

CONTENTS

Grilled Onion and Sumac Lamb Chops,
page 83

INTRODUCTION

Middle Eastern food traditions are integral to my personal and familial history. My paternal grandmother was from Istanbul, and my paternal grandfather migrated from Corfu to Alexandria, Athens, and finally San Francisco. My mother's family was from Crete, and they were farmers in the San Joaquin Valley in California. I grew up hearing stories about my great-uncle's gourmet shop in Istanbul and the bakery of another great-uncle in Alexandria; meanwhile, at home in California, I was eating all the wonderful foods available from the farm.

As the third generation of our family assimilates into American culture, I want to expose them to my childhood foods and show them the hospitality that is so intrinsic to the Middle East and Mediterranean. To keep the cuisine and culture alive, I've adapted recipes to be "user friendly," so they become approachable and easy to incorporate into our daily food rituals. I frequently entertain family and friends for meals. From these joyful gatherings, the idea to share these recipes to other people was born.

I have taken some of my favorite recipes and turned them on their side (so to speak) to create faster versions with all the flavor of the originals. While cuisines of the Old World can seem mysterious and intimidating, truthfully, they focus on simple recipes using fresh and local ingredients. Fortunately, many ingredients that were once exotic are now more readily available, making it much easier to create authentic flavors. In this book, I looked at my favorite Middle Eastern recipes and thought of ways to create those memorable flavors and textures in 30 minutes. When you use what is readily available (canned beans, tomato sauce, etc.) and add traditional spices and herbs, it's easy to create the same satisfying foods to be shared and enjoyed with your family and guests.

In this book, you will find recipes for breakfast, lunch, dinner, dessert, and my favorite, meze or snacks. Many recipes are one-pot or one-pan recipes, and some use only five ingredients (not counting some staples like oil, salt, and pepper). All these recipes are designed to be part of larger meals, and because of their simplicity, they are perfect for entertaining. You can make many of these dishes ahead of time. Knowing you have delicious food on hand, you'll be able to relax and welcome your guests graciously, which is another hallmark of Middle Eastern culture. I'll also provide you with tips throughout this book on how to organize your cooking so that you are more efficient in the kitchen. Middle Eastern flavors will become an easy part of your weeknight rotation, but these tips will serve you no matter what type of cuisine you are cooking.

I hope you will explore these dishes and flavors from throughout the Middle East and keep the tradition of hospitality alive by sharing them with your own family and friends.

Shakshuka,
page 22

Chapter 1

QUICK AND EASY MIDDLE EASTERN COOKING

A conundrum with Middle Eastern food is enjoying these classically slow-cooked meals in a fast-forward world. In this chapter, I'll introduce the kaleidoscope of cultures and ingredients that make up the base of Middle Eastern cuisine and go over many ways to create these authentic flavors and textures in 30 minutes.

Middle Eastern Cuisine and Culture

Middle Eastern cuisine is rich in traditions and flavors. Much of the food from this region is slow food, spiced and marinated, slowly simmered or started the day before. Yogurts and cheeses are strained through cheesecloth for a denser texture, olives and pickles are marinated for days or weeks, and fruits are turned into preserves or dried. These classic preparations were born from the need to preserve foods or make the most of scarce or less-than-perfect ingredients. In spite of this, hospitality is a hallmark of the cuisines of the Middle East, and food is meant to be shared.

REGIONS AND RECIPES

The Middle East is a large geographical area that includes between eighteen and twenty-one countries, depending on who's counting. It's broadly the region between Europe, Asia, and Africa and the Mediterranean, Red, Arabian, and Caspian Seas. The countries and traditions of this region have all contributed their part to the flavors and traditions of this cuisine. Middle Eastern food is akin to Mediterranean food, as both regions share similar diets and healthy lifestyles.

Throughout the Middle East, you will find similar versions of many recipes Baklava, for example, exists in some form from Greece to Morocco, Egypt, Turkey, Iran, and Israel. In Greece, it is made with walnuts and honey, while in Iran it is made with pistachios and sweetened orange syrup. Moussaka is another common dish, with as many variations as there are countries claiming it as their own. Similarly, varieties of yogurts, labneh, and hummus are regularly stocked items on supermarket shelves. These foods now belong to the world, not just their countries of origin. This book is in no way a comprehensive guide to Middle Eastern foods, but rather a personal journey through some of my favorites based on our family recipes and recipes from friends and chefs.

This book includes recipes from throughout the region, including recipes that reflect my own family's ties to Turkey, Cyprus, and Egypt. Additionally, you'll find recipes with Arabic, Iranian, Israeli, Moroccan, Lebanese, and Syrian influences and more, based on my experience working with chefs from these cultures.

SIMPLE STAPLES

The Middle East is an ancient world: one of the first areas to keep farm animals and cultivate plants. Fermentation was developed here. Without fermentation, there wouldn't be yeasted breads, yogurts, cheese, alcohol, and vinegar. Nuts are abundant in this region and figure prominently in many recipes, whether they're ground into a paste and added to dips, sweetened with dates to create desserts, or pressed into oils to flavor vegetables. And let's not forget fruit: beautiful ruby red pomegranate arils glisten like jewels atop of vegetables, yogurt, or meat; and fresh juicy figs are drizzled with olive oil and dusted with ground toasted walnuts.

My cooking philosophy has always been aligned with these principles and emphasizes whole, fresh, seasonal ingredients and good-quality pantry items. For most recipes, produce is easily exchanged for the seasonal equivalent in your part of the world, so don't be afraid to experiment. Rice is a grain eaten throughout the Middle East, along with bulgur and barley. While I love the flavor of basmati rice, any rice will do. Since many cultures in this area don't eat pork, I omitted it in this book, only including recipes with chicken, beef, lamb, seafood, and vegetables.

The Middle East is known for its creativity with simple ingredients. The cuisine is hearty, earthy, and uses a broad range of spices and herbs. Standards include soups and stews made from simple broth bases and vegetables, meats, and beans simmered in spices such as cinnamon, cumin, or paprika. Salads are a mainstay made from seasonal, fresh ingredients or pickled vegetables when the season limits variety. Meats can be grilled for a quick preparation or given a long, slow braise or roast. Many of the dishes that define Middle Eastern cuisine are meze, or appetizers. The spreads, sauces, and small plates create a wonderful variety of easy-to-prepare dishes, and you can even use them as condiments for dinner or sandwiches.

FAST FLAVOR

Because no one has much time to spend on dinner, there are plenty of products to help you along the way. Two of my favorites are frozen and shelf-stable cooked rice. Both are hot and ready in minutes in the microwave. Pita and naan bread are available in most supermarkets; condiments such as harissa, olives, spice blends, and oils are common as well. These ingredients will help you be a pro in the kitchen. For example, I used chickpea flour instead of grinding chickpeas when making Falafel (page 86), and I panfried them for a delicious meal in 30 minutes. If I could shorten the cooking time and maintain the integrity of the dish, I did it. With that in mind, I did not include slow braises or overnight marinades.

VAST VARIETY

When I think of the Middle East, I think of a vibrant mosaic of culinary perspectives. Each country makes the most of local ingredients, creating plant-forward cuisines that don't shy away from using spices. I think of creative cultures using what they have available. Throughout the Middle East, you will see a variety of recipes using spinach, cucumbers, tomatoes, peppers, cabbages, lemons, oranges, and nuts, all showcasing this creativity—and that doesn't even touch on the hundreds of ways to use yogurt.

In this book, you will find universal favorites such as shakshuka from Turkey, kuku from Iran, tabbouleh from Lebanon and Syria, and couscous and tagines from Morocco. Additionally, there are Middle Eastern–ish recipes such as Date and Walnut Muffins (page 29) and Spiced Lamb and Pine Nut Pita Pizzas (page 82). These recipes take advantage of classic Middle Eastern ingredients and meld them into dishes that are both traditional and modern.

MEZE

Meze is one of my favorite words, right up there with dessert. The word orig-inated from the Turkish word for snack or appetizer, which came from the Persian word *mazzah*, meaning "taste." The word has many spellings throughout the Middle East and the Mediterranean. In my family, we called them *mezethes*. But they are also known as *mezzeh, mezze,* or *mazza*.

There are no rules about what to serve; any snack served before the main meal can be called a meze. Typically, meze is served cold or at room temperature, but hot dishes can include Kibbeh (page 73), Chicken "Kebabs" (page 66), and savory pastries such as Cheese Borek (page 34). Cold meze can be as simple as a hearty chunk of feta cheese generously drizzled with olive oil and herbs and served with thick slices of country bread. Common meze in Greece include feta, olives, cucumbers, stuffed grape leaves (not a 30-minute recipe, but available in grocery stores and ethnic markets), and spreads such as Hummus (page 39) and Toum (page 119). In other parts of the Middle East, meze may also feature cheese (white cheese, Halloumi, feta, or labneh), flatbread, and fruit such as melon. However, in some areas, meze is a more progressive meal, beginning with olives, tahini, salad, and yogurt, followed by a variety of salads and egg dishes, then small meat dishes, and finally more substantial whole fish or grilled meats.

In Muslim regions, meze is served without alcohol; in places such as Greece, Turkey, Lebanon, and the Balkans, meze is usually served with drinks. If enjoying meze in a region where alcohol is allowed, you can expect to be served pun-gent raki, licorice-flavored ouzo, robust red wine, resin-flavored mastika, and other local beverages.

All these various types of meze have the same goal: to bring people around the table to taste, relax, and prepare their appetite for the meal ahead. Because of the importance of meze, there is a chapter dedicated to it. I suggest Hummus (page 39), Cucumber-Mint Yogurt Sauce (page 124), Pita Chips (page 125), Baba Ghanouj (page 41), Roasted Vegetables with Baharat (page 45), and Cracked Green Olives with Garlic and Onions (page 47). However, you can easily create a last-minute meze party with no cooking at all with a well-stocked pantry. Keep olives, roasted red peppers, pickled vegetables, tinned fish, and tinned dolma in the pantry and some hard cheese or feta in the refrigerator, and you're ready to go.

Maximize Your 30 Minutes

The skills you will learn in this section will serve you well no matter what you're cooking. The Middle East is known for its slow-cooked stews and soups, rotisserie meats, and marinated roasts, and there's nothing like these dishes when time allows. But by using canned beans, broths, ground meat, spice blends, and fresh herbs, similar results are achievable in under 30 minutes of cooking time.

PREP RIGHT

Being prepared and having a game plan is the best way to achieve success, especially if you're new to cooking or unfamiliar with Middle Eastern food. These ingredient prep techniques will help make things go smoothly when you get down to the cooking.

CUTTING AND CHOPPING

When you move quickly in the kitchen, cutting and chopping can be a balance of priorities. Diced or minced ingredients cook the fastest but take the longest to cut. I suggest using a rough chop for most vegetables and keeping the pieces under ½ inch for quick cooking. Another way to save time is to slice vegetables ¼ inch thick instead of chopping—this works especially well with root vegetables.

If you aren't skilled with a knife, I suggest buying a selection of vegetables to practice on and then throwing all your handiwork into a stockpot, adding water or broth, and cooking up a pot of vegetable soup.

If you have time to cut vegetables ahead of cooking, that's great. I have found reusable containers with snap-on lids to be excellent for keeping chopped vegetables fresh for a long time. You can cube meat and poultry and store it the same way, but it's best to use meat within 24 hours of prepping. Prep fish shortly (less than an hour) before using. In this book, I've kept the cut size for most proteins around 1 inch or smaller for ease of cooking. If cutting meat into 1-inch cubes, it's easier to use very cold meat. Cut the larger piece into 1-inch slices, then stack two slices together and cut into 1-inch cubes.

For vegetables, cut them into small dice. It's easier if you first cut a very thin strip off the vegetable so that it lays flat, then cut it into slices, cut the slices into strips, and cut the strips into a small dice. A coarse chop will work for onions, tomatoes, and herbs.

Many vegetables can be sliced widthwise into coins, or in the case of larger vegetables like zucchini and cucumbers, halved lengthwise and cut into slices or half-moons. Because of its pungency, garlic should be minced or thinly sliced.

When cutting vegetables for a salad, it's fine to tear greens into largish pieces or use wedges of tomatoes or cucumbers, but keep the pieces fork-size for ease of eating.

MEASURING

Unless you are baking, measuring doesn't have to be exact for most ingredients, as long as it's close. A little extra broth, tomato sauce, yogurt, or herbs won't matter that much, so if you make a mistake, don't worry about it. The recipes in this book are very forgiving.

You can experiment with soups and stews, but be aware that many of the spices in this book are robust and it's best to under-season and add more later than to over-season. Cinnamon, cloves, peppers, garlic, vinegar, and salt can easily overwhelm other ingredients. For desserts, sugar, honey, and cinnamon can completely take over the flavor profile of a recipe. Baking isn't as forgiving, and it's best to follow the recipes closely, because too much flour or too much liquid can completely ruin a dessert.

If you don't have measuring cups and spoons, you can still get by using the following tips: Use a small water glass to measure 1 cup, a kitchen spoon to measure 1 tablespoon, and several pinches to measure 1 teaspoon. A cut of meat about the size of your palm will be about 4 ounces.

COOKING SHORTCUTS

You can speed up some dishes with a bit of planning. You can save lots of cooking time with whole grains if you soak them in water for several hours, ideally overnight, before you cook them. To soak them, place the amount of grains you want to cook in a jar, add water to cover the grain by 2 inches, cover, and refrigerate until you're ready to cook. Then drain the grains, discard the water, and cook them as described in the recipe.

Parboiling is a great technique if you're cooking beans from a dry state and you don't have any time to soak them. Place the beans in a pot, cover them with water by 2 inches, and bring them to a boil; simmer for 30 to 45 minutes, drain, discard the water, and rinse the beans. Then cook the beans as described in the recipe.

TIME-SAVING COOKING STRATEGIES

Even if you haven't nailed your prep, there are plenty of ways to cheat time in the kitchen. The following strategies can help you quickly get everything from the stove to the table.

USE APPLIANCES

Middle Eastern cuisine is not traditionally appliance heavy, but certain tools will make quicker work of some recipes.

Ideally, I suggest a blender or a food processor. They both have specific uses, but a blender will suffice if you can only have one. A food processor can quickly chop meats and vegetables, making it a great tool for meatballs. A food processor and blender will make short work out of salad dressings, spreads, and sauces. An immersion blender is great for pureeing soups right in the cooking pot. A handheld mixer is helpful for whipping eggs or cream, as well as for making batters.

A microwave is good for defrosting foods or melting butter. It can also be used to "parboil" grains, beans, or potatoes. Just place them in water and microwave for 5 minutes. Strain and discard the water, and continue cooking as described in the recipe. This jump-starts the cooking process for ingredients that are usually time-consuming to prepare.

Pressure cookers, multifunction cookers, and slow cookers are great to have. The classic slow cooker is a working family's friend, since you can set it up in the morning and come home to a cooked meal. Pressure cookers and multifunction pots are lovely because they pack lots of usefulness into one countertop appliance. And it's true—many things taste better when cooked in a pressure cooker.

BUY FRESH (AND FROZEN)

I live in an area abundant in fresh seasonal fruits and vegetables. If you live in an agricultural area, and if time allows, prep produce and place it in food storage containers or bags until you need it. Most fruit can be cut, placed in a single layer on a parchment paper–lined baking sheet, and frozen; once frozen, you can keep the fruit in a food storage container in the freezer until needed.

Fortunately, many markets sell precut produce; if your market is one of them, take advantage. Precut options will often be in the produce section or frozen vegetables section.

Frozen vegetables are great helpers when time is short. If using thawed vegetables, strain them to remove the extra liquid before cooking so that your dish doesn't become watery.

For those who don't have fresh produce available, frozen fruits and vegetables are perfectly fine and, in some cases, more nutritious than their fresh counterparts. I was thrilled to see frozen fava beans in the market. Shelling fava beans is a chore; now, all I have to do is cut open a bag.

When I plan my weekly meals, I create a shopping list, get what I need, and prep what I can as soon as I get home. If the recipe has a tomato-based sauce (such as Shakshuka, page 22, for instance), go ahead and cook the sauce for a quick-to-assemble dish the next day. Tomato-based dishes always taste better the next day. Or make cold sauces such as Tahini Sauce (page 118) or Harissa Paste (page 122) ahead. You can make most of the desserts in advance.

Some of the recipes in this book, such as Baba Ghanouj (page 41) and Lamb and Tomato Soup (page 57), can be made in bigger batches and frozen in single servings for a quick reheat. Others, like Cheese Borek (page 34), can be frozen uncooked, ready to pop in the oven whenever you're ready to prepare them. Don't overwhelm yourself; plan for the fewest number of meals you need to get through the week.

PLAYING FAST AND LOOSE WITH LOW AND SLOW

Slow cooking is a reliable method for getting a lot of flavor from a few ingredients, but it takes time! And while using appliances like a slow cooker or pressure cooker can't magically bring a stew onto your dinner table in under 30 minutes, they can make it easier and somewhat faster than stovetop cooking. You can adapt some of the recipes, like White Bean and Beef Soup (page 60), for a pressure cooker. Set the pressure cooker for 20 minutes at high pressure, and you'll have soup in about 40 minutes once the pressure builds, cooks, and releases. If using a pressure cooker for this recipe, you can also use 1-inch cubes of lamb instead of ground lamb for a more traditional stew.

Almost any stew or soup in this book can be made in a slow cooker for a longer cook but more hands-off time. Slow cookers are great for replicating the flavors of the North African cooking pot, the tagine. Any of the tagine recipes in this book can be cooked in a slow cooker on high for 2 hours or for 6 hours on low instead of in a pot on the stove.

The Efficient Middle Eastern Kitchen

A well-stocked kitchen will make cooking Middle Eastern dishes much easier. You'll have confidence that ingredients are available without checking the pantry or shop for every meal. While some of the ingredients may initially be unfamiliar to you, I think you'll find that they will become go-to staples as you get to know them and incorporate them into your cooking routine.

INGREDIENT STAPLES

I always keep these essential ingredients on hand, and they will be used frequently throughout the recipes in this book.

SPICES

Spices create the unique flavors of Middle Eastern cooking, and the combination of spices in each blend will indicate the origins of the recipe.

For instance, Baharat (page 121) is from Tunisia, and Advieh Spice Blend (page 123) is from Iran. Although both blends have some of the same spices, each uses them in a slightly different way.

When possible, purchase the freshest spices you can find, ideally from a spice shop. However, if the supermarket is your only option, buy the smallest container they sell since spices lose flavor over time.

Once you are comfortable with the flavors of the suggested spices, feel free to create your own mixes.

Cardamom, ground: Cardamom grows in seed-containing pods. The seeds are removed and then ground. It's used a lot throughout the Middle East and India.

Cinnamon, ground: Cinnamon is one of the granddaddy spices throughout the Middle East and the Mediterranean. It is used in both sweet and savory dishes.

Cloves, ground: Cloves are very pungent and should be used in small amounts. You may be tempted to skip them, but don't; cloves add depth of flavor.

Coriander, ground: Coriander is the dried seed of cilantro, and the flavor is similar but more intense.

Garlic powder: Every kitchen should have garlic powder on hand; it's a kitchen staple. Don't be heavy-handed with it—a little goes a long way.

Ginger powder: Like cinnamon, ginger is used in both sweet and savory dishes.

In the Middle East, dried ginger is used more frequently than fresh ginger.

Paprika: There are several types of paprika. The classic kind is the one someone sprinkled over potato salad or deviled eggs when you were growing up. There's also sweet paprika, hot paprika, and smoked paprika. I prefer sweet paprika, which allows me to control how spicy I want to make my dish. Smoked paprika is also great, not too hot, with a delicious smoky flavor.

Peppercorn blend or black peppercorns: I prefer a blend of pepper, but if you can only find black, that's fine, too. Always use freshly ground for the best flavor.

Red pepper flakes: Red pepper flakes are an easy way to add a little kick to a recipe. Add a pinch or two, depending on how spicy you like it.

Salt, kosher and sea: These are my preferred salts for cooking as they have much milder saltiness and a more complex flavor than table salt.

Turmeric, ground: Recently the modern world has discovered turmeric's anti-inflammatory properties, but our ancestors knew about that all along. Turmeric is a tad sour and adds a lovely orange/gold glow to every dish.

PANTRY

These shelf-stable goods are my favorites to have around and help create the backbone of a Middle Eastern meal. Your market may not carry some of these items, but they all can easily be found online.

Beans: Chickpeas, lentils, gigantes, and white beans are available cooked—both canned or in vacuum-packed pouches—which don't require soaking and cooking like dried beans.

Bulgur: Bulgur is cracked wheat that reconstitutes quickly with boiling water. It has many uses, including as a base for a salad or pilaf or as a thickener for Kibbeh (page 73).

Honey: Honey in the Middle East is darker, richer, and thicker than the honey in our markets. In the store, look for orange blossom honey or sample different honeys at the farmers' market to find your favorite.

Nuts: Almonds, walnuts, and pistachios are the most frequently used. If you can't find shelled pistachios, use almonds instead.

Olive oil: Used throughout the Middle East, Mediterranean, and Southern Europe, the best oil is whichever one you like. I look for organic extra-virgin olive oil. Many olive oils in our markets come from Spain and Turkey, so you may be using Turkish olive oil without even knowing it.

Olives: It's easy to keep a variety of olives on hand. If possible, buy pitted olives to save time in the kitchen.

Pomegranate molasses: Pomegranate molasses might be tricky to find in your store; it can be in the condiments section or with the sugars and syrups. Save yourself some time and ask a staff person. If it's not available, you can make a reasonable substitution with balsamic vinegar (pomegranate balsamic, if they have it) and honey.

Red wine vinegar: Red wine vinegar has a sharp, robust flavor that is distinctive in many of the salads of the Middle East.

Roasted red peppers: Roasted red peppers are handy as part of a meze table, but they are also a perfect quick addition to Shakshuka (page 22) and soups.

Tahini: This sesame paste is readily available near the nut butter in most markets. I find the imported brands to have a more authentic flavor than the brands that are sold as a spread or nut butter.

Tomato puree: Tomato sauce makes stew taste like stew and adds a sweet-tart flavor to recipes. Try different brands and find one you like; varieties can run the gambit from very acidic to slightly acidic. I always get plain tomato puree or a basic marinara so that I can season it to complement what I'm cooking.

FRESH AND REFRIGERATED

These perishable ingredients are always in my refrigerator so I can throw together something at a moment's notice. Other than meats and seafood, most items will last for 7 to 10 days.

Carrots: Good ol' carrots add sweetness to soups, roast beautifully when dusted with a spice blend, and are refreshing shredded into a salad.

Chicken thighs: Buy boneless, skinless chicken thighs. They cook quickly and are almost impossible to overcook, so keep a few packages in the freezer.

Eggs: Eggs are used throughout this book as a part of breakfast or baked goods. I like organic pasture-raised large eggs.

Fresh herbs: Fresh herbs are a hallmark of Middle Eastern cooking. I suggest having Italian parsley, mint, and thyme. Fresh herbs will last longer if you wrap a damp paper towel around the stems and place them in an airtight container or resealable plastic bag.

Frozen spinach: Fresh and frozen spinach is used frequently in Middle Eastern cooking, and I suggest keeping both on hand. Thaw frozen spinach and drain as much liquid as possible from it before proceeding with the recipe.

Garlic: I always have two heads of garlic on hand, because you just never know.

Ground lamb: Ground lamb may not be readily available, but lamb stew meat usually is. You can ask the butcher to grind it for you, or you can finely chop it in a food processor.

Onions: Yellow and red onions are most commonly used in this book.

Pita or naan bread: In addition to enjoying these breads as a side to a meal, you can easily make them into pizzas and sandwiches, filling them with bits and pieces of leftover dishes. I suggest buying these fresh and keeping some on hand in the freezer.

Yogurt: It's best to purchase plain whole-milk Greek yogurt. Some recipes call for labneh, which may be harder to find; Greek yogurt is a good substitute.

TOOLS AND EQUIPMENT

Like a well-stocked kitchen, good tools will make your life much easier. You won't need anything fancy—unless you want it.

MUST-HAVE

These are the absolute essentials you'll want to have to make most of the recipes in this book.

12-inch skillet: This is an item you don't need to break the bank for. Cast-iron and green pans (non-stick pans with a ceramic coating) are very reasonably priced and easy to find. Ideally, look for one that is oven-safe for dishes that start on the stove and finish in the oven.

Baking sheet: It's easy to make quick meals when using a baking sheet, as the flat surface allows the food to cook rapidly. Buy the type that has a rim, so the juices don't flow onto the oven floor.

Blender: If you want to make Hummus (page 39) or Harissa Paste (page 122) from scratch, this is a must-have tool, but, though there are so many blenders to choose from, there's no need to buy a high-end machine.

Bowls: A set of nesting bowls will handle most of your needs. It's a good idea to have a set of three bowls—small, medium, and large—but if you can only purchase one bowl, get an 8-inch one (about 2 quarts).

Casserole or baking dish: In order to save time, it will be very helpful to have a dish that can go from oven to table. It can be as simple as an oven-safe glass 8-inch square dish, a 9-by-13-inch pan, or a lovely ceramic casserole dish.

Dutch oven: A Dutch oven is an absolute must-have for soups and stews. However, a top-of-the-line cast-iron enameled pot is not necessary—any 4- to 7-quart pot with a lid will suffice. They're great for stews, soups, and pastas, and they can go from stove to oven to table.

Knives: All you need is a paring knife, an 8-inch chef's knife, and a serrated bread knife. This trio is often sold in kits, and you can often find them on sale.

Ladle: Nothing gets soup or stew out of a pot better than a ladle.

Measuring cups and spoons: Get a set of dry measuring cups, wet measuring cups, and measuring spoons.

Spatulas: A rubber-tipped spatula is the ideal tool for mixing and removing food from a bowl. Look for one that's heat safe. A metal offset spatula is handy for flipping eggs or fish and for removing cakes and pies from their pans.

Strainer: A fine-mesh wire strainer is essential for straining foods or removing solids from broth.

Vegetable peeler: Peelers are not only handy for peeling fruits and vegetables, but they can be an excellent tool for shaving cheese.

Whisk: A whisk makes short work of beating eggs and smoothing sauces.

NICE TO HAVE

If you have the space in your kitchen and you are becoming a cooking pro, here are some items that are nice to have.

Food processor: The wider bowl of a food processor makes it ideal for chopping vegetables, grinding meats, or making doughs.

High-powered blender: A high-powered blender will make short work of grinding nuts, turning grains or nuts into flours, and pureeing sauces.

Mandoline: There are inexpensive plastic mandolines on the market that are excellent for thinly slicing vegetables for salads and sandwiches.

Microplane: Microplanes are very fine graters that are excellent for zesting citrus or adding a shower of cheese to a dish.

Mixer: A stand mixer is fantastic, but if you don't have the space, a handheld mixer will get the job done in recipes like Middle Eastern Shortbread Cookies (page 115).

Sharpening steel: Regularly using a steel will keep your knives sharp in between professional sharpening.

Spice grinder: Freshly ground spices will take your food to the next level. When using a spice grinder with multiple spices, it's best to grind some saltines after each spice to clean out the machine.

SHOPPING AND SOURCING

While most of the ingredients called for in this book can be found in any grocery store, specialty food stores, delis, and gourmet supermarkets are your best bet to locate some of the less common ingredients. You can also easily find most nonperishable items online.

SPECIALTY INGREDIENTS

Specialty ingredients can be hard to locate in markets. If you have a Middle Eastern market in your area, make use of it. When shopping in a supermarket or big box store, ask staff members for help locating specific items; it will save you time.

Except for olive oils and perishable items like proteins and yogurts, it's best to purchase imported ingredients for these recipes. Using pantry items from the Middle East will add special, authentic flavors and textures to your dishes.

Some stores have a gourmet aisle and/or an international aisle; those are two places to look for specialty ingredients. Fortunately, global ingredients are easier to locate now that everything can be found online. What is not available online may be available at Whole Foods, Trader Joe's, or other gourmet grocery stores.

SUBSTITUTIONS

If I'm unable to find a specialty ingredient, I look for a good substitute or create a facsimile. Greek yogurt is everywhere now, but there was a time when I would strain traditional yogurt to create it. Or, as I mentioned earlier, if you can't find pomegranate molasses, you can make something similar with 2 parts balsamic vinegar and 1 part honey.

BEST FIRST STEPS

To get the most out of this book and make the first steps in your Middle Eastern cooking journey a breeze, I recommend paring things down at the start. First, choose a few recipes to try—I suggest two to five dishes. Get familiar with the methods and flavors, and then move on to expand your repertoire. Choose which day you plan to prepare each dish.

Make a shopping list, checking your pantry items and dry goods and adding any fresh ingredients needed. If time allows, prep as much as you can ahead of time; for example, prep your vegetables as soon as you get home from the store as you put them away. Read through the recipe before you begin cooking.

If you don't have time to cook a full recipe, stock your pantry with the suggested items in the pantry section and make some of the spice mixes or sauces included in chapter 8. A standard chicken dinner will have a Middle Eastern flair if the chicken is seasoned with Advieh Spice Blend (page 123), served with rice and roasted vegetables, and topped with Toum (page 119). Lamb chops can be made special when they are served with Tahini Sauce (page 118) and potatoes roasted with Za'atar (page 120).

About the Recipes

And now to the good stuff! The recipes in this book are designed to give you the essence of Middle Eastern cuisine with just 30 minutes in the kitchen, based on my personal and familial history with these culinary traditions and my experience working with chefs from around the region.

In many cases, I've given you classic recipes that can be easily made in 30 minutes, such as Turkish Eggs (page 24) and Israeli Couscous Salad (page 38). Elsewhere I have modified the techniques or ingredients of the original dish to make it quicker to prepare, like Baklava Tartlets (page 111), or a little easier to source, like the Advieh Spice Blend (page 123). I've also included some recipes I love that are Middle Eastern in spirit—or Middle Eastern–inspired—such as Yogurt Pancakes with Honeyed Apricots (page 20) and Breakfast Pitas with Harissa and Fried Eggs (page 32). Some recipes are a complete meal, while others can be combined to create a meal—I've included serving suggestions for pairing recipes. Try Turkish Bulgur Salad (page 50) and Chicken "Kebabs" (page 66) if you can't decide where to start.

I've included substitutions for hard-to-find ingredients and cooking technique and storage tips throughout the recipes. And although many religions throughout the Middle East have dietary rules and guidelines, I have not conformed to any of these specific traditions, so be aware that you may need to make certain substitutions if you need to adhere to those guidelines.

LABELS

For ease of use, the recipes in this book are labeled with the following:

5-Ingredient: For recipes that use just 5 ingredients, excluding salt, pepper, and oil

No-Cook: For recipes that don't require heat or cooking time

One-Pot: For recipes made entirely in one pot or pan (e.g., a Dutch oven, rimmed baking sheet, or skillet)

Vegetarian/Vegan: For recipes that don't include animal protein (Vegetarian), dairy, honey, or other animal products (Vegan)

TIPS

In addition to the recipe labels, you'll find tips that expand on the information provided in the recipes:

Did You Know? An interesting ingredient fact, historical/cultural context, or cooking tip

Make-Ahead Tip: Throughout the book, I'll let you know what parts of the recipe can be made ahead

Substitution Tip: Different ingredients that can be used if ones called for in the recipe are unavailable

Serving Tip: Suggestions for toppings, side dishes, and main courses that pair beautifully with the recipe

Storage Tip: How long a recipe will last in the refrigerator or freezer

Variation Tip: When possible, I'll note what changes can be made to make a recipe vegan instead of vegetarian or suggest alternative ingredients to accommodate other dietary restrictions

Kuku (Iranian Frittata),
page 26

Chapter 2

EGGS AND BRUNCHES

Yogurt Pancakes with Honeyed Apricots

SERVES 4 ♦ **PREP TIME:** 10 minutes ♦ **COOK TIME:** 15 minutes

Yogurt—an integral ingredient throughout the Middle East and the Mediterranean—makes moist, delicate pancakes because of its fermentation and richness. One theory of the origin of yogurt concerns shepherds from Turkey placing milk in sheepskin bladders for easy transport. The bladder's environment promoted fermentation and thickened the milk. Prep the dry and wet ingredients separately the night before to make your morning easier, cover them, and store the dry mixture on the counter and the wet mixture in the refrigerator. When you are ready to make the pancakes, combine the two to mix up the batter. I use fresh apricots in this recipe, but any stone fruit or berry will do. You can also substitute labneh or kefir for the yogurt.

8 ounces apricots, pitted and cut into quarters

4 tablespoons sugar, divided

½ teaspoon ground cinnamon

2 cups all-purpose flour

1½ teaspoons baking powder

1½ teaspoons baking soda

1 teaspoon kosher salt

2 cups plain whole-milk Greek yogurt

2 large eggs

2 tablespoons extra-virgin olive oil

½ teaspoon almond extract

Melted butter or oil, for greasing the pan

½ cup honey

1. In a small bowl, combine the apricots, 2 tablespoons of sugar, and the cinnamon and mix until the apricots are evenly coated. Set them aside.

2. In a large bowl, combine the flour, the remaining 2 tablespoons of sugar, the baking powder, the baking soda, and the salt, whisking until blended.

3. In a medium bowl, combine the yogurt, eggs, olive oil, and almond extract and whisk until smooth.

4. Add the wet ingredients to the dry and mix with a spatula until well blended.

5. Heat a large skillet or griddle until hot. Grease with butter or oil and reduce the heat to medium.

6. Spoon about ⅓ cup of the batter onto the griddle or skillet for each pancake and cook until bubbles appear on the surface, 3 to 5 minutes.

7. Use a spatula to flip the pancakes and cook until golden, 3 to 4 minutes.

8. Stack the pancakes onto a serving dish, top with the apricots and honey, and serve immediately.

Cooking Tip: Cook only a few pancakes at a time; don't overcrowd the pan. You can keep pancakes warm by placing them on a baking sheet in a medium-low (200°F) oven. To make these vegan, use an almond milk yogurt and egg replacement, and substitute maple syrup for the honey.

Shakshuka

SERVES 4 ♦ PREP TIME: 10 minutes ♦ **COOK TIME:** 15 minutes

Shakshuka is a dish made of a simple sauce of onions, red peppers, and tomatoes, with eggs poached directly in the sauce. It is excellent with fresh or canned tomatoes, making it a year-round staple. You can eat it any time of the day, but shakshuka is often enjoyed for breakfast. I would serve this with thick slices of rustic country bread or Pita Chips (page 125) for dipping.

3 tablespoons extra-virgin olive oil, divided

1 small yellow onion, diced

1 garlic clove, sliced

1½ teaspoons smoked paprika or sweet paprika

½ teaspoon ground cumin

1 (14½-ounce) can peeled whole tomatoes

Pinch red pepper flakes

1 teaspoon kosher salt

4 large eggs

2 ounces feta cheese, crumbled (optional)

1 tablespoon coarsely chopped fresh parsley

1. In a large skillet over high heat, warm 2 tablespoons of olive oil.

2. Add the onion and garlic and sauté until the garlic is fragrant, about 3 minutes. Add the paprika and cumin and sauté to toast the spices, about 1 minute.

3. Add the tomatoes and their juices, the red pepper flakes, and the salt and bring to a simmer. Use a spoon or spatula to break up the tomatoes into 2-inch pieces.

4. Use the back of a spoon to make four wells in the sauce and gently crack an egg into each of the wells.

5. Cover the skillet, reduce the heat to medium, and cook until the eggs are cooked to your preference, about 5 minutes for runny yolks or 8 minutes for firm yolks.

6. Remove the lid, garnish with the feta (if using) and parsley, and drizzle with the remaining 1 tablespoon of olive oil.

Substitution Tip: If tomatoes are in season, use them instead of canned tomato sauce. Roma tomatoes are the easiest choice. Make an X on the bottom of each tomato with a sharp knife. Bring a medium pot of water to a boil over high heat and place each tomato in the boiling water until the skin loosens from the flesh, 2 to 3 minutes. Remove the tomatoes with a slotted spoon, peel them when they are cool enough to handle, and remove and discard the stem ends. Place the peeled tomatoes in a blender and puree. Proceed with the recipe as written. It will take approximately 1 pound of fresh tomatoes to make the equivalent of 1 (14½-ounce) can of tomato puree.

Turkish Eggs

SERVES 4 ♦ **PREP TIME:** 10 minutes ♦ **COOK TIME:** 15 minutes

Turkish eggs is a very simple dish of eggs served over a garlicky yogurt sauce and drizzled with spiced brown butter and herbs. In this recipe, we use Toum for the sauce along with Harissa Paste, a red chili condiment. Traditional Turkish eggs feature poached eggs, but this version using fried eggs is easier to master and a bit quicker to cook. This meal is a creamy, spicy, garlicky delicious mess best enjoyed with a thick slab of toasted bread. I promise it will become one of your favorite breakfasts.

2 cups Toum (page 119)

FOR THE SPICED BUTTER

8 tablespoons
   (1 stick) butter

2 teaspoons Harissa
   Paste (page 122) or
   store-bought harissa,
   plus more to taste

¼ teaspoon ground cumin

¼ teaspoon
   smoked paprika

FOR THE EGGS

2 tablespoons butter

4 large eggs

¼ teaspoon kosher salt

1 tablespoon finely
   chopped fresh dill

1 tablespoon finely
   chopped fresh parsley

1. Divide the toum between four serving dishes, swirling it on each plate and creating nests for the eggs.

TO MAKE THE SPICED BUTTER

2. In a small skillet over high heat, melt the butter.

3. Once the butter has melted, swirl it in the skillet until it starts to brown, 2 to 3 minutes. Once the butter has browned, remove the skillet from the heat.

4. Add the harissa, cumin, and paprika and whisk to combine, then set aside.

5. In a large skillet, melt the butter over high heat.

6. Crack the eggs into the skillet, keeping them separated. Reduce the heat and cover the skillet. Cook until they reach your desired doneness, 5 to 8 minutes.

7. Place 1 egg on top of the toum on each plate.

8. Divide the spiced butter between the plates and sprinkle each egg with salt.

9. Garnish each plate with the dill and parsley and serve immediately.

Variation Tip: Instead of fried eggs, for foolproof poached eggs, crack each egg into a fine-mesh strainer, letting the additional egg white drip through. Gently transfer the egg to a ramekin and repeat with each egg. Place a medium saucepan filled with 2 inches of water over medium heat and bring to just under a boil. Add 1 tablespoon of white vinegar to the water. Gently tip each egg into the simmering water, keeping them separate. Cover with a lid, turn off the heat, and let the eggs sit for 5 to 8 minutes. Gently remove each egg with a slotted spoon, touch the spoon bottom to a paper towel to absorb excess water, and serve.

Did You Know? Straining eggs before poaching them removes all the stringy bits of egg white, leaving a nicely shaped oval.

Kuku (Iranian Frittata)

SERVES 4 ♦ PREP TIME: 15 minutes ♦ **COOK TIME:** 10 minutes

Kuku is a mixture of herbs and eggs baked into a pancake, much like a frittata. Its hallmark is the quantity of greens in the mix—lots and lots of herbs. But it can also include spinach, zucchini, beet tops, or other vegetables, so feel free to swap in whatever you have on hand. Because chopping herbs is time-consuming, I combine all the ingredients in a blender or food processor for easy prep. Traditionally, kuku is served with a garlicky yogurt sauce like Toum (page 119) or a dab of Harissa Paste (page 122), and it can be eaten hot or at room temperature.

1 bunch Swiss chard or spinach, cut into 1-inch pieces, leaves only

½ bunch fresh parsley, coarsely chopped

½ bunch dill, coarsely chopped

½ bunch mint, coarsely chopped

2 scallions, white and green parts, thinly sliced

1 garlic clove

6 large eggs

1 tablespoon all-purpose flour

½ teaspoon ground turmeric

½ teaspoon kosher salt

¼ teaspoon freshly ground black pepper

2 tablespoons butter

1. Preheat the oven to 400°F.

2. Place the Swiss chard, parsley, dill, mint, scallions, and garlic in a blender or food processor and pulse several times to chop coarsely.

3. Add the eggs, flour, turmeric, salt, and pepper and process until just combined. Don't over-blend, or it will look like a green smoothie.

4. In a large skillet over high heat, melt the butter.

5. Gently pour the mixture into the skillet and cook for 1 to 2 minutes, until the bottom begins to set.

6. Carefully place the skillet in the oven and cook for 8 to 10 minutes, until the eggs are cooked through.

7. Cut into 4 to 6 wedges and serve.

Cooking Tip: To make this without a blender or food processor, finely chop the chard, parsley, dill, mint, and scallions. Combine the eggs, flour, turmeric, salt, and pepper in a medium bowl and whisk until combined. In a large oven-safe skillet, melt the butter, add the chard and herbs, and sauté for about 1 minute to wilt. Pour the egg mixture over the greens and bake as outlined in the recipe.

Couscous with Dried Fruits and Cinnamon

SERVES 4 TO 6 ♦ **PREP TIME:** 10 minutes ♦ **COOK TIME:** 5 minutes

Although treated as a grain, couscous is a pasta made from semolina wheat flour and water, shaped into grain-size pieces, and dried. It is easily reconstituted in hot water and is ready to eat in minutes. Although couscous is common in savory dishes in the United States, serving it with cinnamon and dried fruits is a nice change from the usual breakfast cereals. You can also enjoy this dish warm with a dollop of yogurt or a splash of cream.

1 cup golden couscous

1¼ cups boiling water

½ teaspoon kosher salt

2 tablespoons butter

½ cup dried apricots, quartered

½ cup dried cherries

3 tablespoons sugar

½ teaspoon ground cinnamon

¼ cup chopped pistachios or another nut (optional)

1. Place the couscous in a large bowl. Add the boiling water and salt and cover. Let the couscous sit for 5 minutes, then fluff with a fork.

2. In a small skillet over medium-high heat, melt the butter. Add the apricots, cherries, sugar, and cinnamon and sauté until the fruit plumps, 2 to 3 minutes.

3. Add the fruit to the couscous and mix to combine.

4. Spoon the couscous into serving dishes, garnish with pistachios (if using), and serve.

Ingredient Tip: There are several varieties of couscous; this recipe uses speedy golden couscous. Israeli or pearl couscous must be simmered in water for 10 minutes, until tender. You can use these varieties but cook them first. Olive oil can be substituted for butter to make this dish vegan.

Date and Walnut Muffins

MAKES 12 MUFFINS ◆ PREP TIME: 10 minutes ◆ **COOK TIME:** 20 minutes

This recipe incorporates dates and olive oil for a Middle Eastern flavor profile and an extremely moist muffin. To save time, try combining the dry ingredients in a large bowl ahead of time and add the wet ingredients shortly before baking. Purchase chopped pitted dates, or at least pitted ones. Dried figs also work well, and almonds can stand in for the walnuts. One of these muffins with tea is a lovely afternoon break.

½ cup hot water

½ cup pitted
   chopped dates

⅓ cup honey

2 large eggs, beaten

¼ cup extra-virgin olive oil

1 teaspoon vanilla extract

2 cups all-purpose flour

2 teaspoons
   baking powder

1 teaspoon baking soda

1 teaspoon ground
   cinnamon

1 teaspoon kosher salt

½ cup chopped walnuts

1. Preheat the oven to 375°F. Line a 12-cup muffin tin with paper liners.

2. In a large bowl, pour the hot water over the dates and mash with a fork to mix. Add the honey and stir to combine.

3. Add the eggs, olive oil, and vanilla and stir to combine. Add the flour, baking powder, baking soda, cinnamon, and salt and mix well. Fold in the walnuts.

4. Scoop the batter by ½-cup scoops into the prepared pan.

5. Bake until lightly browned, 15 to 20 minutes.

6. Let the muffins cool for 5 minutes before eating.

Storage Tip: Store these muffins at room temperature for several days in an airtight container, or store them in the freezer for several months.

Did You Know? Even though dates look like dried fruit, they are, in fact, fresh fruit. Medjool dates are the most popular date in North America because of their size and sweet, velvety texture. Dates have trace amounts of vitamins and are a good source of fiber.

Ful Mudammas

SERVES 4 TO 6 ♦ **PREP TIME:** 10 minutes ♦ **COOK TIME:** 10 minutes

This fava bean stew is the Egyptian breakfast of champions. Fava beans, also known as broad beans, are large, fleshy, bright green beans loaded with protein and fiber. However, they are a chore to prepare. The beans must be removed from their pods, and the tough outer shell must be peeled off. Thankfully, they are available canned and frozen. The beans are seasoned here with cumin, garlic, red pepper flakes, and lemon juice and are traditionally garnished with condiments like chopped tomatoes, cucumbers, scallions, and olives. It's also perfect unadorned, served with pita bread. If you like spicy food, add Harissa Paste (page 122).

2 (15-ounce) cans
fava beans, drained
and rinsed

½ cup water or
vegetable broth

1 garlic clove, sliced

½ teaspoon kosher salt

½ teaspoon ground cumin

Pinch red pepper flakes

Juice of 1 lemon

¼ cup extra-virgin olive oil

OPTIONAL GARNISHES

½ cup diced tomato

½ cup diced cucumber

2 scallions, white and
green parts, thinly sliced

2 tablespoons finely
chopped fresh parsley

Pita or naan bread,
for serving

1. In a large skillet over medium heat, combine the beans, water, garlic, and salt.

2. Bring to a simmer and cook, stirring frequently until the garlic is aromatic, about 2 minutes.

3. Add the cumin and red pepper flakes and mash the mixture with the back of a spoon. It doesn't have to be smooth; just break down the beans to make a soupy texture.

4. Once the beans are partially mashed, turn off the heat and add the lemon juice and olive oil. Stir to combine.

5. Serve hot with garnishes of your choice or on its own with pita or naan bread.

Ingredient Tip: Frozen fava beans are available in some markets. If using frozen fava beans, cook them according to the package directions before using them in this recipe. Any large bean will work if you can't find fava beans. This dish can be made the night before and reheated in the morning or frozen for several months in individual portions.

Breakfast Pitas with Harissa and Fried Eggs

SERVES 4 ♦ PREP TIME: 15 minutes ♦ **COOK TIME:** 10 minutes

This recipe is Middle Eastern–ish with its pita-and-harissa base, and it's what I imagine as the precursor to the fast-food breakfast sandwich. These toasted pitas are topped with fried eggs, feta, and harissa to make an open-faced sandwich eaten by hand or with a knife and fork for a quick, easy, and satisfying breakfast. If you don't have the time to make Harissa Paste, it's available in many markets and online. Keep pita in your freezer, so you can enjoy this whenever the mood strikes.

4 pita breads

½ cup extra-virgin olive oil, divided

1 garlic clove, crushed

8 large eggs

1 to 2 tablespoons Harissa Paste (page 122) or store-bought harissa

1 scallion, white and green parts, thinly sliced

¼ cup feta, crumbled (optional)

1. Preheat the oven to 400°F.

2. Place the pita breads on a baking sheet (you may need two baking sheets depending on the size of the pitas). Brush the pitas with ¼ cup of olive oil and rub them with the crushed garlic.

3. Bake until lightly browned, 5 to 6 minutes.

4. While the pitas toast, heat the remaining ¼ cup of olive oil in a large skillet over medium-high heat.

5. Crack the eggs into the skillet, keeping them separated. Reduce the heat to medium, cover, and cook until they reach your desired doneness, 5 to 8 minutes.

6. Place 2 eggs on each pita and garnish with harissa paste, scallions, and feta (if using) and serve hot.

Variation Tip: For a high protein breakfast without eggs, substitute Hummus (page 39) for the eggs—and omit the feta to make it fully vegan.

Spiced Lamb Scramble

SERVES 6 TO 8 ♦ **PREP TIME:** 10 minutes ♦ **COOK TIME:** 15 minutes

This scramble is another Middle Eastern–inspired spin on a breakfast staple. It starts with ground lamb, cooked with onions, mint, and Baharat (see tip), then eggs are scrambled in, and the scramble is served garnished with nuts. I also like to add a dollop of labneh and eat it with Pita Chips (page 125). Although eggs are a classic breakfast food, many cultures that raise and consume chickens will eat eggs throughout the day.

2 tablespoons extra-virgin olive oil

1 small onion, finely chopped

1 garlic clove, minced

1 teaspoon Baharat (page 121)

1 pound lean ground lamb

4 large eggs, beaten

1 tablespoon finely chopped mint

2 tablespoons toasted pine nuts or chopped almonds

½ teaspoon kosher salt

1. In a large skillet over high heat, warm the olive oil. Add the onion and garlic and sauté until softened, about 2 minutes. Add the baharat and cook until aromatic, about 30 seconds.

2. Crumble the lamb into the skillet and cook until browned and no longer pink, 5 to 8 minutes.

3. Pour the eggs into the skillet and scramble for 2 to 3 minutes.

4. Remove from the heat and add the mint, pine nuts, and salt. Serve hot.

Substitution Tip: If you're unable to make Baharat, you can season this dish with ½ teaspoon of ground allspice and ¼ teaspoon of smoked paprika for a quick substitute. You can make the lamb mixture the night before; reheat it in the skillet, and add the eggs to finish the dish the next day.

Cheese Borek

SERVES 6 TO 8 ♦ **PREP TIME:** 15 minutes ♦ **COOK TIME:** 15 minutes

Borek or *bourekas* are savory pastries filled with meat, vegetables, or cheese. You can make them with phyllo or puff pastry—in my family, the puff pastry is considered more Turkish, and phyllo is more Greek-style. Typically, borek are a small, handheld size. However, I often make them as one larger rectangular pie and serve it cut into squares to speed things up. One of my favorite ways to enjoy Cheese Borek for breakfast is to drizzle it with honey and serve it with good strong coffee.

2 sheets frozen store-bought puff pastry, defrosted but cold

1 large egg, beaten

1 (15-ounce) container ricotta cheese

²/₃ cup feta cheese, crumbled

1 large egg yolk

Pinch kosher salt

Pinch freshly ground black pepper

1 tablespoon sesame seeds

1. Preheat the oven to 400°F. Line a baking sheet with parchment paper.

2. Place one sheet of puff pastry on the baking sheet. Brush around the perimeter of the puff pastry with the beaten egg.

3. In a small bowl, combine the ricotta, feta, egg yolk, salt, and pepper and mix well.

4. Transfer the ricotta mixture to the puff pastry, gently spreading it out and leaving at least a 1-inch border.

5. Place the second sheet of puff pastry on top, lining up the edges with the bottom sheet of puff pastry, and use a fork to crimp the edges.

6. Use a sharp knife to make a ½-inch cut on the top of the pie for the steam to escape.

7. Brush the pastry with the remaining beaten egg and sprinkle with the sesame seeds.

8. Place in the oven and bake until golden, approximately 15 minutes.

9. Let rest for 5 minutes, then cut into 6 or 8 squares before serving.

Variation Tip: Use any combination of ricotta and Middle Eastern or Mediterranean soft white cheeses, such as goat cheese or manouri. Parsley and mint are nice additions to the filling. Borek can be assembled a day ahead of time and refrigerated to bake whenever you are ready.

Tabbouleh,
page 44

Chapter 3

MEZE AND SMALL PLATES

Israeli Couscous Salad

SERVES 6 TO 8 ♦ **PREP TIME:** 15 minutes ♦ **COOK TIME:** 15 minutes

Like its smaller counterpart, Israeli couscous is made from semolina. It is sometimes called pearl couscous because the grains are shaped like pearls. Their larger size means you have to boil them before using, unlike traditional couscous, which is simply reconstituted with boiling water. However, Israeli couscous makes a more toothsome, textured salad, so it is worth the extra work. You can find Israeli couscous at specialty or gourmet markets and online. This salad is a great side for roasted meats or grilled fish.

- 6 tablespoons extra-virgin olive oil, divided
- 1 cup Israeli couscous
- 1¼ cups water
- 1 teaspoon kosher salt, divided
- Juice and grated zest of 1 lemon
- 1 English cucumber, cut into ½-inch pieces
- 1 cup cherry tomatoes, halved
- ¼ cup coarsely chopped fresh cilantro
- ¼ cup coarsely chopped fresh dill
- ¼ teaspoon freshly ground black pepper

1. In a medium saucepan over medium-high heat, warm 2 tablespoons of olive oil.

2. Add the couscous and sauté to lightly toast it, 2 to 3 minutes.

3. Add the water and ½ teaspoon of salt and bring to a boil.

4. Reduce the heat to medium, cover, and cook until the couscous is tender, about 10 minutes. Drain any excess cooking liquid.

5. Place the couscous in a medium bowl and use a spoon or fork to fluff the grains.

6. Add the lemon juice, lemon zest, cucumber, tomatoes, cilantro, dill, the remaining 4 tablespoons of olive oil, the remaining ½ teaspoon of salt, and the pepper and fold to mix.

7. Place in a serving dish and serve warm or at room temperature.

Variation Tip: You can add chickpeas, feta, roasted vegetables, or nuts to this salad. It's best when eaten within 48 hours.

Hummus

MAKES ABOUT 2 CUPS ♦ PREP TIME: 15 minutes

We always made hummus at my restaurant jobs during the 1980s; at that time, it was considered exotic, so it wasn't available at the market or from wholesale vendors. Hummus is really easy to make, especially with a food processor. Using Tahini Sauce will add flavor and texture, but if you don't have time to make it, regular tahini works well. Like natural nut butter, tahini separates in the jar, so be sure to stir it up before using.

1 (15-ounce) can chickpeas, drained and rinsed

¼ cup freshly squeezed lemon juice

¼ cup tahini or Tahini Sauce (page 118)

¼ cup extra-virgin olive oil

1 garlic clove, sliced

½ teaspoon kosher salt

½ teaspoon ground cumin

1. Place the chickpeas, lemon juice, tahini, olive oil, garlic, salt, and cumin in a food processor.

2. Pulse several times to chop and then let the machine run until the mixture is very smooth, stopping to scrape the sides of the bowl down frequently.

3. If the mixture is too thick, add ice water, 1 tablespoon at a time, until you reach your desired consistency.

4. Transfer to a serving dish and serve.

Variation Tip: Hummus will taste better if allowed to sit for 30 minutes before serving. You can substitute white beans or fava beans for the chickpeas. Try garnishing your Hummus with chopped roasted red peppers, Harissa Paste (page 122), or chopped roasted beets. Store covered in the refrigerator for up to 10 days.

Labneh and Mint with Pita Chips

MAKES ABOUT 2 CUPS ♦ **PREP TIME:** 15 minutes

Labneh is a thick, cultured dairy product more like cream cheese than yogurt. It's strained like Greek yogurt, but the flavor is tangier, so it suits savory dishes better than sweet. I have seen it in the dairy case at my local grocery store and Middle Eastern markets. If you aren't able to find it, Greek yogurt is a good substitute. This dish is enjoyed throughout the Middle East, and additions like spinach or cucumbers are common. I like Pita Chips with this dip, but warm pita bread is also delicious.

1 cup labneh

1 garlic clove, minced

1 tablespoon extra-virgin olive oil

2 tablespoons finely chopped fresh mint

¼ teaspoon kosher salt

Pinch red pepper flakes

Pita Chips (page 125), for serving

1. In a small bowl, combine the labneh, garlic, and olive oil and mix until smooth.

2. Add the mint and salt and mix well.

3. Transfer to a serving dish and garnish with the red pepper flakes.

4. Serve with the pita chips for dipping.

Serving Tip: This dip will taste better if allowed to sit for 30 minutes before eating.

Storage Tip: Refrigerate in an airtight container for up to 4 days.

Baba Ghanouj

MAKES ABOUT 2 CUPS ♦ **PREP TIME:** 15 minutes ♦ **COOK TIME:** 10 minutes

Like hummus, baba ghanouj is one of those recipes found throughout the Middle East with many variations. This eggplant spread can include tomatoes or not, and the eggplant can be sliced and roasted or roasted whole and scooped out. The best baba ghanouj I ever had was made by an Egyptian chef who deep-fried the eggplant instead of roasting it. Since most of us don't deep-fry at home, I developed a panfried version.

¼ cup extra-virgin olive oil

1 garlic clove, sliced

1 large eggplant, peeled and cut into 1-inch cubes

2 tablespoons Tahini Sauce (page 118) or store-bought tahini

½ teaspoon kosher salt

¼ teaspoon freshly ground black pepper

1 tablespoon freshly squeezed lemon juice

1 tablespoon finely chopped fresh parsley

1. In a large skillet over high heat, warm the olive oil. Add the garlic and sauté until aromatic, about 30 seconds.

2. Add the eggplant and cook, stirring occasionally until it is very soft and lightly caramelized, 5 to 8 minutes.

3. Turn off the heat and add the tahini sauce, salt, and pepper and use a spoon or potato masher to mash the mixture until it's spreadable but still has texture.

4. Add the lemon juice and mix well. Transfer to a serving bowl and garnish with the parsley.

Substitution Tip: If you can't find a large globe eggplant, substitute three Asian eggplants instead. I think it's best eaten warm or at room temperature. Refrigerate in an airtight container for up to 5 days.

Did You Know? Even though we associate eggplant with the Middle East and the Mediterranean, it is grown globally. It is a fruit, not a vegetable, and it contains an amino acid that helps reduce anxiety and promote good sleep.

Pickled Vegetables

MAKES ABOUT 2 CUPS ◆ **PREP TIME:** 15 minutes ◆ **COOK TIME:** 5 minutes

Cucumbers and onions are the vegetables most commonly pickled in the Middle East, but you can use this technique to pickle carrots, green beans, cauliflower, and peppers as well. This recipe calls for Persian cucumbers, but regular or English cucumbers will also work well. When packing the vegetables, use a container that allows them to be completely submerged in the pickling liquid. Once the vegetables have softened a bit in the warm liquid, you can push them down and add more liquid. If using a larger jar, shake the contents daily to submerge all the vegetables.

2 cups sliced
   Persian cucumber
   (¼-inch slices)

½ small red onion, cut
   into ¼-inch slices

1 garlic clove, sliced

1 teaspoon
   coriander seeds

1 teaspoon fennel seeds

FOR THE PICKLING LIQUID

1 cup water

1 cup white vinegar

3 tablespoons sugar

2 teaspoons kosher salt

1. Place the cucumber, onion, garlic, coriander seeds, and fennel seeds in a 1-quart canning jar.

2. To make the pickling liquid, in a small saucepan, combine the water, vinegar, sugar, and salt over medium heat and stir until the sugar has dissolved, 3 to 5 minutes.

3. Pour the pickling liquid over the vegetables, making sure they are completely submerged in the liquid.

4. Cover and let sit at room temperature for at least 15 minutes before eating. The longer the vegetables pickle, the better they will taste.

5. Refrigerate for up to 10 days.

Serving Tip: The crunch and acidity of these pickles complement the smooth textures of yogurt and Hummus (page 39), and they can cool the spiciness of Harissa Paste (page 122).

Muhammara

MAKES ABOUT 1½ CUPS ♦ **PREP TIME:** 15 minutes

Muhammara is a favorite dip throughout the Middle East; the name comes from the Arabic word *ahmar*, which means red. This dish is believed to have originated in Syria in the city of Aleppo, and I used Aleppo pepper in this recipe. I also used pomegranate molasses, which can be easily purchased online. If you can't locate the molasses, substitute a mixture of 2 parts balsamic vinegar with 1 part honey. Muhammara has a thick texture and is stellar as a sandwich spread or as a dip for raw vegetables.

1 cup roasted red peppers

½ cup toasted walnuts, coarsely chopped

1 scallion, white and green parts, coarsely chopped

1 garlic clove, sliced

¼ cup extra-virgin olive oil, plus more for garnish

2 tablespoons pomegranate molasses

1 teaspoon ground cumin

1 teaspoon kosher salt

¼ teaspoon Aleppo pepper flakes (or more to taste), plus more for garnish

½ cup breadcrumbs

1. Place the peppers, walnuts, scallion, and garlic in a food processor or blender and pulse several times until finely chopped.

2. Add the olive oil, pomegranate molasses, cumin, salt, and Aleppo pepper flakes and puree until smooth. Add the breadcrumbs and process until smooth.

3. Transfer to a serving dish, make a well in the center, and garnish with olive oil and Aleppo pepper flakes.

4. Refrigerate in an airtight container for up to 5 days.

Cooking Tip: To toast your own walnuts, place the walnuts on a baking sheet in a 400°F oven (or toaster oven) and bake until lightly toasted, 5 to 6 minutes. Alternatively, place the walnuts in a dry skillet over medium-high heat and stir frequently until lightly toasted, about 5 minutes. If you can't find Aleppo pepper flakes, substitute red pepper flakes.

Tabbouleh

SERVES 4 TO 6 ◆ PREP TIME: 15 minutes

Tabbouleh is a traditional Middle Eastern salad made with bulgur wheat, a cracked and parboiled whole grain. Like couscous, bulgur only needs boiling water to make it tender and fluffy. Bulgur is thought to originate from Turkey and is considered one of the oldest processed foods. This salad is generously seasoned with olive oil, lemon juice, and herbs. As it sits, the bulgur absorbs the flavors, so it's better to over-season this salad; the flavors will mellow between preparation and serving. I only use a single bunch of parsley in this recipe, but feel free to increase the herbs to your liking, or add a handful of raisins for a pop of sweetness.

½ cup bulgur

1¼ cups boiling water

1 cup diced cucumber

1 cup cherry
    tomatoes, halved

2 scallions, white and
    green parts, thinly sliced

1 teaspoon kosher salt

1 bunch fresh
    parsley, chopped

1 bunch fresh
    mint, chopped

Juice of 2 large lemons

⅓ cup extra-virgin olive oil

1. In a large bowl, combine the bulgur and boiling water, cover, and let it sit until the bulgur is tender, 15 to 20 minutes. Drain any excess liquid and fluff the bulgur with a fork.

2. Add the cucumber, tomatoes, scallions, and salt and mix well.

3. Add the parsley, mint, lemon juice, and olive oil and mix until combined.

4. Transfer to a serving dish and serve.

Ingredient Tip: Bulgar is typically sold as bulgur wheat and can be labeled fine, medium, coarse, or extra-coarse. Do not use extra-coarse for this recipe. I've included the soaking step, but alternatively, you can follow the directions on the package. Because there is a large quantity of herbs, you can save time by chopping them in a food processor. It's best to eat tabbouleh within 48 hours of preparation, and it is best enjoyed at room temperature.

Roasted Vegetables with Baharat

SERVES 4 TO 6 ◆ PREP TIME: 10 minutes ◆ **COOK TIME:** 20 minutes

Baharat is a Tunisian spice mix that blends the sweet and savory flavors loved throughout North Africa and the Middle East. This blend is composed of easy-to-find spices, but it can also be purchased online or at a spice shop. I love roasting root vegetables like these with Baharat and serving them with a dollop of labneh or Greek yogurt. They make an excellent meze, or they are delicious alongside grilled or roasted meats or fish when served without the yogurt.

4 large carrots, cut into ½-inch slices

2 large parsnips, peeled and cut into ½-inch slices

1 cup cauliflower florets

1 small red onion, cut into ¼-inch slices

¼ cup extra-virgin olive oil

1 tablespoon Baharat (page 121) or store-bought

1 teaspoon kosher salt

1. Preheat the oven to 400°F.

2. In a large bowl, combine the carrots, parsnips, cauliflower, and onion.

3. Add the olive oil and mix to coat the vegetables.

4. Add the baharat and salt and mix well.

5. Spread the vegetables in a single layer on a rimmed baking sheet and roast until tender, 15 to 20 minutes.

6. Serve warm or at room temperature.

Variation Tip: Any seasonal vegetable is great with Baharat. Many stores sell prepared cubed winter squashes, cauliflower florets, and trimmed green beans. Additionally, I like to add zucchini and fennel. This recipe will last for about 1 week in the refrigerator.

Rolled Flatbread Sandwiches

MAKES 12 ROLLS ♦ PREP TIME: 15 minutes

Known as aram sandwiches, these are the hit of every meze table. Aram sandwiches are attributed to Armenia and are made with lavash, a flatbread made by toasting very thin dough sheets to make large rectangles or pizza-size round crackers. Lavash is enjoyed throughout the Middle East, and it is sold ready to use in the deli, bakery, bread aisle, or frozen aisles of most grocery stores. You can order it online as well. If you can't find lavash, you can use pita pockets.

2 pieces traditional lavash rectangles

8 ounces Hummus (page 39) or store-bought

1 cup sliced roasted red peppers, patted dry (about 5 ounces)

2 scallions, white and green parts, thinly sliced

½ cup crumbled feta

4 cups baby spinach

1. Place one of the lavash rectangles on a work surface.

2. Spread with half of the hummus and top with half of the red peppers, half of the scallions, half of the feta, and half of the spinach.

3. Tightly roll up the bread in jelly-roll fashion, place it seam-side down, and set it aside.

4. Repeat the process with the remaining piece of lavash.

5. Allow the rolls to sit for 10 minutes before slicing so they hold their shape.

6. Slice each roll into 6 pieces, arrange on a platter, and serve.

Ingredient Tip: If the lavash is dry, it needs to be softened with damp towels to make it pliable enough to roll. If time allows, wrap the rolls in plastic wrap and refrigerate for 30 to 60 minutes before serving to allow the flavors to develop fully. These sandwiches are almost infinitely adaptable: You can use Muhammara (page 43) instead of the Hummus, or try adding chopped Pickled Vegetables (page 42) and chopped olives.

Cracked Green Olives with Garlic and Onions

MAKES 1 POUND ♦ **PREP TIME:** 10 minutes

For most of my childhood, a 5-gallon bucket of olives sat curing on our back porch. Once, out of curiosity, I tried an olive fresh off the tree, and it was terrible! I don't know what compelled the ancient world to devise a way to eat them, but I'm glad they did. With this simple recipe, olives are even more delicious. I like to use green olives, but any type will work. The flavored marinating oil is also delicious as a dip for bread.

1 pound olives with pits

½ cup extra-virgin olive oil

¼ small yellow onion, sliced

1 garlic clove, sliced

1 rosemary sprig

1 strip orange peel about ½ inch wide by 2 inches long

1. Use the flat side of a knife to crack the olives lightly.

2. Place the olives in a jar or airtight food storage container.

3. Add the olive oil, onion, garlic, rosemary, and orange peel. The oil should cover the olives completely, so add more oil if necessary.

4. Allow the mixture to sit for 20 minutes before serving.

Variation Tip: Pitted olives aren't right for this recipe since they are mushy when cracked. Another version of this dish uses dry, cured olives with oregano instead of green olives and rosemary. The longer they marinate, the better. Store the olives in the refrigerator for up to 2 weeks.

Did You Know? Olives spread throughout the Middle East and the Mediterranean over 6,000 years ago and are the oldest known cultivated tree. There are over 200 varieties of olives in the world, but only about 150 varieties are commonly cultivated.

Lentil Soup,
page 56

Chapter 4

SOUPS AND SALADS

Turkish Bulgur Salad

SERVES 4 TO 6 ♦ **PREP TIME:** 20 minutes ♦ **COOK TIME:** 5 minutes

This Turkish grain salad is like Tabbouleh (page 44), but it is made with a cooked tomato and red pepper sauce instead. I think of it as both a salad and a side dish because it can be served warm and is a bit saucy. To make it more salad-y, I will add chopped vegetables or chickpeas at the end. I love serving it with the Grilled Onion and Sumac Lamb Chops (page 83).

1 cup bulgur

3 cups boiling water

¼ cup extra-virgin olive oil

1 garlic clove, sliced

1 cup store-bought tomato sauce

½ cup minced roasted red peppers

1 teaspoon kosher salt

3 scallions, white and green parts, thinly sliced

⅓ cup chopped fresh parsley

2 tablespoons store-bought pomegranate molasses

½ teaspoon ground cumin

1. Place the bulgur in a large bowl, add the boiling water, cover, and let sit until tender, 15 to 20 minutes. Use a fork to fluff the bulgur and set it aside.

2. In a large skillet over high heat, warm the olive oil. Add the garlic and sauté until aromatic, about 30 seconds. Add the tomato sauce and roasted red peppers and bring to a simmer.

3. Add the tomato sauce and salt to the bulgur and stir until it is evenly coated with the sauce. Add the scallions, parsley, pomegranate molasses, and cumin and mix well.

4. Serve warm or at room temperature.

Substitution Tip: You can substitute marinara sauce for the tomato sauce.

Storage Tip: Refrigerate this salad in an airtight container for up to 5 days.

Lebanese Lentil Salad

SERVES 4 TO 6 ♦ PREP TIME: 15 minutes

This salad is made from lentils, bulgur, and lots of herbs. High in fiber and protein, it's a nutrition powerhouse that is wonderful on its own. You can stuff it into a pita with a dollop of Toum (page 119) or Harissa Paste (page 122) or serve it as a side dish with baked fish. This dish is often enjoyed at potluck events since it tastes best at room temperature.

½ cup bulgur

1¼ cups boiling water

1 (15-ounce) can lentils, drained and rinsed

¼ cup extra-virgin olive oil

2 garlic cloves, minced

¾ cup chopped fresh parsley

¾ cup chopped fresh mint

1 teaspoon kosher salt

Juice of 1 lemon

½ teaspoon ground cumin

¼ teaspoon ground allspice

Freshly ground black pepper

1. Place the bulgur in a large bowl, add the boiling water, cover, and let sit until tender, 15 to 20 minutes. Use a fork to fluff the bulgur.

2. Add the lentils and olive oil and mix well.

3. Add the garlic, parsley, mint, salt, lemon juice, cumin, and allspice, season with pepper, and mix to combine.

4. Transfer to a serving dish and serve.

Variation Tip: This dish is supposed to be very garlicky, so add more to suit your taste. Other additions could include cucumber, tomato, and feta.

Storage Tip: Refrigerate this salad in an airtight container for up to 4 days.

Did you Know? Lentils are edible legumes that grow in pods. There are many varieties, such as green, brown, yellow, red, and black. They are high in fiber and protein, so they are important for a healthy diet. Black lentils are the most nutritious, with ½ cup of cooked black lentils containing 18g of fiber and 26g of protein.

Fattoush

SERVES 4 TO 6 ◆ **PREP TIME:** 15 minutes

This bread salad is one of my absolute favorite things to eat. It combines crunchy Pita Chips, with vegetables and a dressing that soaks into the bread for a perfectly soft yet crunchy texture. Traditionally, the pita are fried, but the baked chips work just as well; you can even use store-bought pita chips to make this salad a real cinch. Once the Pita Chips have been added, you should eat the salad within several hours or the texture will go from delightful to soggy.

1 head romaine, chopped

1 cup cherry
    tomatoes, halved

1 cup cucumber, diced

1 red bell pepper,
    seeded and diced

½ cup sliced radishes

2 scallions, white and
    green parts, sliced

¼ cup chopped
    fresh parsley

¼ cup extra-virgin
    olive oil

1 garlic clove, minced

2 teaspoons red
    wine vinegar

1 teaspoon kosher salt

4 ounces Pita Chips
    (page 125) or
    store-bought

Freshly ground
    black pepper

1. In a large bowl, combine the romaine, tomatoes, cucumber, bell pepper, radishes, scallions, and parsley.

2. In a small bowl, combine the olive oil, garlic, red wine vinegar, and salt and whisk to blend.

3. Pour the dressing over the vegetables and toss to mix.

4. Add the pita chips and mix well, and season to taste with black pepper.

5. Transfer to a serving dish and serve.

Make-Ahead Tip: You can make the salad up to the point of adding the pita chips, several hours ahead. If Pita Chips aren't available, substitute torn pieces of pita bread.

Carrot Salad

SERVES 4 TO 6 ♦ PREP TIME: 15 minutes

Carrot Salad is a fond childhood memory of mine, as it was an easy way for my mom to get us kids to eat vegetables. She would make it with carrots, red wine vinegar, extra-virgin olive oil, salt, and pepper. She kept it simple to appeal to our child taste buds, but my version is seasoned with Baharat to give it a Moroccan flavor. I love eating it as a side dish with Chicken and Apricot Tagine (page 67) or Whole Roasted Spiced Fish (page 97). If rainbow carrots are in season, use them for an even more colorful dish.

1 pound carrots, shredded

¼ cup chopped
   fresh cilantro

1 scallion, white and
   green parts,
   finely chopped

½ cup extra-virgin olive oil

3 tablespoons freshly
   squeezed lemon juice

½ teaspoon Baharat
   (page 121) or
   ground cumin

½ teaspoon kosher salt

Pinch red pepper flakes

Freshly ground
   black pepper

1. In a medium bowl, combine the carrots, cilantro, and scallion.

2. In a small bowl, whisk the olive oil, lemon juice, baharat, salt, and red pepper flakes to blend.

3. Pour the dressing over the vegetables and toss to mix.

4. Season to taste with pepper and serve.

Variation Tip: To make this a more substantial salad, I like to add chickpeas and currants.

Storage Tip: Refrigerate in an airtight container for up to 5 days.

Beet Salad with Pomegranate Molasses and Pistachios

SERVES 4 TO 6 ◆ PREP TIME: 15 minutes

I love this composed salad for its brilliant colors and the rich flavor of the beets with pomegranate molasses. It is delicious and beautiful on the plate. Using store-bought cooked beets makes this salad substantial and super quick. You can find them in the produce section of your grocery store or substitute canned or pickled beets. I've used shaved ricotta salata on this salad, but any hard cow's or sheep's milk cheese works well.

1 (5-ounce) package arugula

½ pound cooked beets, cut into ½-inch cubes

½ small red onion, thinly sliced

¼ cup shelled pistachios

3 tablespoons extra-virgin olive oil

1 tablespoon pomegranate molasses

2 teaspoons red wine vinegar

½ teaspoon kosher salt

Freshly ground black pepper

¼ cup pomegranate arils (optional)

¼ cup shaved ricotta salata

1. Arrange the arugula on a serving platter or divide it between 4 individual plates.

2. Arrange the beets, red onion, and pistachios on the arugula.

3. In a small bowl, whisk together the olive oil, pomegranate molasses, red wine vinegar, salt, and pepper.

4. Drizzle the dressing over the salad.

5. Garnish with the arils (if using) and ricotta salata and serve.

Substitution Tip: To make this salad vegan, omit the ricotta salata. Pomegranate arils are available in the produce section of most grocery stores. If you can't find them, you can substitute dried cranberries or barberries, a sweet-tart dried fruit often used in Iranian cooking and available online.

Cabbage with Herbed Citrus Yogurt

SERVES 4 TO 6 ♦ PREP TIME: 15 minutes

Sumac is a dark red, pungent spice with a lemony tart flavor. Sumac is a flowering plant related to the cashew plant and is grown throughout the world, including in East Asia, Africa, and North America. It is popular throughout the Middle East and Mediterranean and is excellent in spice rubs, salads, or brewed into a tea. If you can't find it, this salad will still be delicious without it and pairs wonderfully with roast chicken.

1 (10-ounce) package shredded green cabbage

3 scallions, white and green parts, thinly sliced

1 cup plain whole-milk Greek yogurt

½ cup mayonnaise

¼ cup extra-virgin olive oil

3 tablespoons freshly squeezed lemon juice

1 garlic clove, minced

2 tablespoons chopped fresh mint

1 tablespoon grated lemon zest

½ teaspoon sumac

½ teaspoon kosher salt

Freshly ground black pepper

1. In a large bowl, mix the cabbage and scallions to combine.

2. Add the yogurt, mayonnaise, olive oil, lemon juice, garlic, mint, lemon zest, sumac, salt, and pepper. Mix until the ingredients are well blended.

3. Transfer to a serving dish and serve.

Serving Tip: You can make the dressing several days ahead of time and dress the salad shortly before serving. Once dressed, the salad should be eaten within 48 hours because as it sits, the dressing will become runny and you might have to drain the excess liquid.

Lentil Soup

SERVES 4 TO 6 ♦ **PREP TIME:** 10 minutes ♦ **COOK TIME:** 20 minutes

Lentil soup is a mainstay throughout the world. Lentils are grown globally and are inexpensive, nutritious, and satisfying. Lentils are believed to have been the first legume ever cultivated, and they originated in the Middle East. This soup can become a stew with more vegetables, chicken, or meat; in some parts of the Middle East, diced potatoes are added. Perfect as is, this dish is also delicious with a dollop of labneh or Harissa Paste (page 122).

¼ cup extra-virgin olive oil

1 small onion, diced

2 garlic cloves, minced

1 teaspoon ground cumin

¼ teaspoon cayenne pepper

6 cups water or vegetable broth

12 ounces yellow or red lentils, rinsed and picked through

⅓ cup chopped fresh cilantro

¼ cup freshly squeezed lemon juice

1 teaspoon kosher salt

1. In a large pot over medium-high heat, warm the olive oil.

2. Add the onion and garlic and sauté until the vegetables are soft, about 5 minutes. Add the cumin and cayenne and sauté to toast the spices, about 30 seconds.

3. Add the water and lentils and bring to a boil. Reduce the heat to low and simmer until the lentils are tender, about 15 minutes. The soup should be thick.

4. Turn off the heat and add the cilantro, lemon juice, and salt and mix well.

5. If the soup is too thick, thin it out with a little hot water.

Make-Ahead Tip: This simple, hearty soup is great to have on hand; make a double batch and keep it in the freezer for a future meal.

Storage Tip: Refrigerate leftovers in an airtight container for up to 5 days.

Lamb and Tomato Soup

SERVES 4 TO 6 ♦ **PREP TIME:** 10 minutes ♦ **COOK TIME:** 20 minutes

There are versions of this soup throughout the Middle East. Some versions include rice; others include lentils, chickpeas, or bulgur. Traditionally it is made with lamb stew meat, but this version uses ground lamb to cut the cook time down. This hearty soup only needs a simple salad to make it a complete meal.

½ cup extra-virgin olive oil, divided

1 onion, diced

2 garlic cloves, minced

2 teaspoons sweet paprika

1 teaspoon ground cumin

½ teaspoon ground cinnamon

1 pound ground lamb

1 (15-ounce) can crushed tomatoes

1 quart chicken or beef broth

1 tablespoon honey

1 teaspoon kosher salt

¼ teaspoon freshly ground black pepper

⅓ cup chopped fresh cilantro

1 cup plain whole-milk Greek yogurt

1. In a large pot over medium-high heat, warm ¼ cup of olive oil. Add the onion and garlic and sauté until the vegetables are soft, about 5 minutes. Add the paprika, cumin, and cinnamon and sauté to toast the spices, about 30 seconds.

2. Add the lamb and cook, stirring frequently to brown, about 5 minutes. Add the tomatoes, broth, honey, salt, and pepper and bring to a boil.

3. Reduce the heat to low and simmer to develop the flavors, about 10 minutes.

4. Add the cilantro. Ladle the soup into serving bowls, garnish with the yogurt, drizzle with the remaining ¼ cup of olive oil, and serve.

Variation Tip: Many cooked grains are available in the grocery store's frozen section, so feel free to add cooked brown rice or other grains for a thicker soup.

Ash

SERVES 6 TO 8 ♦ PREP TIME: 15 minutes ♦ **COOK TIME:** 15 minutes

Ash means "thick soup" in Farsi. Traditionally it is eaten as part of a New Year celebration. You can make it with any assortment of vegetables, beans, herbs, and pasta. Ash is usually made with Persian soup noodles—a thin spaghetti-like egg noodle known as reshteh, which is available online or in Middle Eastern shops—but vermicelli or angel-hair pasta are also excellent. Add a dollop of yogurt and/or Harissa Paste (page 122) and a thick slice of bread to sop up all the goodness.

¼ cup extra-virgin olive oil

1 onion, diced

2 garlic cloves, minced

1 teaspoon ground turmeric

1 teaspoon sweet paprika

1 (15-ounce) can chickpeas, drained and rinsed

1 (15-ounce) can kidney beans, drained and rinsed

6 cups vegetable broth or water

1 teaspoon kosher salt

¼ teaspoon freshly ground black pepper

3 ounces Persian soup noodles or angel-hair pasta

2 cups baby spinach leaves

⅓ cup chopped fresh cilantro

⅓ cup chopped fresh parsley

¼ cup chopped fresh dill

2 tablespoons freshly squeezed lemon juice

1. In a large pot over high heat, heat the olive oil. Add the onion and garlic and sauté until softened, 3 to 5 minutes. Add the turmeric and sweet paprika and sauté until aromatic, about 30 seconds.

2. Add the chickpeas, kidney beans, broth, salt, and pepper and bring to a boil. Add the noodles and boil until the noodles are tender, 6 to 8 minutes.

3. Turn off the heat and add the spinach, cilantro, parsley, dill, and lemon juice and mix well.

4. Ladle the soup into bowls and serve.

Ingredient Tip: I specify sweet paprika here, but smoked or hot paprika are equally delicious.

Storage Tip: This recipe makes a large quantity, so freeze half in single-serving containers for days when you need dinner in a hurry. Refrigerate in an airtight container for up to 5 days.

White Bean and Beef Soup

SERVES 4 TO 6 ♦ **PREP TIME:** 10 minutes ♦ **COOK TIME:** 20 minutes

Known as fasoolia baida, which translates to "white bean" in Arabic, this recipe is enjoyed throughout the Middle East. It is typically a combination of meat chunks and white beans, slowly braised in tomato sauce. My 30-minute version replaces the chunks with ground beef and the aromatic broth is packed with fennel, celery, and lots of herbs. This soup is wonderful with any type of bean or with ground lamb or turkey. I like to serve this with a simple green salad or Persian Spiced Cauliflower (page 96).

½ cup extra-virgin olive oil, divided	2 garlic cloves, minced	1 teaspoon kosher salt
1 onion, diced	1 pound (85% lean) ground beef	¼ teaspoon freshly ground black pepper
1 fennel bulb, trimmed and diced	1 (15-ounce) can white beans, drained	⅓ cup chopped fresh parsley
2 celery stalks, diced	1 quart beef broth	¼ cup chopped fresh dill

1. In a large pot over high heat, warm ¼ cup of olive oil. Add the onion, fennel, celery, and garlic and sauté until softened, 3 to 5 minutes.

2. Add the ground beef, break it up with a spoon, and cook until it is browned and no longer pink, 5 to 8 minutes.

3. Add the white beans, broth, salt, and pepper and bring to a boil. Reduce the heat to low and simmer to develop the flavors, 5 to 8 minutes.

4. Turn off the heat, add the parsley and dill, and mix well.

5. Ladle the soup into bowls, drizzle with the remaining ¼ cup of olive oil, and serve.

Cooking Tip: If you want a leaner soup, brown the beef in a separate skillet and drain the fat before adding the meat to the soup.

Storage Tip: Refrigerate in an airtight container for up to 5 days, or freeze for up to 2 months.

Moroccan Chicken Soup

SERVES 4 TO 6 ♦ PREP TIME: 10 minutes ♦ **COOK TIME:** 20 minutes

Inspired by the flavors of a tagine, this soup is satisfying and nutritious. Traditionally, this dish is made with a whole chicken simmered in the soup, removed, and the meat shredded back into the soup. My version uses chicken thigh meat for a much quicker meal. This fragrant tomato broth with Moroccan spices, tender pieces of chicken, and chickpeas is very satisfying on a cold day. I like to serve it with a side of rice or bulgur.

4 tablespoons
(½ stick) butter

1 onion, diced

1 garlic clove, minced

1 small jalapeño pepper,
seeded and chopped

2 teaspoons Baharat
(page 121)

1 pound boneless, skinless
chicken thighs, cut
into 1-inch pieces

1 (15-ounce) can
chickpeas, drained
and rinsed

1 quart chicken broth

1 (8-ounce) can
tomato sauce

1 teaspoon kosher salt

¼ teaspoon freshly
ground black pepper

¼ cup chopped
fresh parsley

1. In a large pot over high heat, melt the butter. Add the onion, garlic, and jalapeño and sauté until softened, 3 to 5 minutes. Add the baharat and sauté until aromatic, about 30 seconds.

2. Add the chicken and cook until browned on all sides, 5 to 8 minutes. Add the chickpeas, broth, tomato sauce, salt, and pepper and bring to a boil.

3. Reduce the heat to low and simmer to develop the flavors and thoroughly cook the chicken, 5 to 8 minutes.

4. Turn off the heat, add the parsley, and mix well. Ladle into bowls and serve.

Substitution Tip: If you don't have Baharat, substitute the following: ½ teaspoon of paprika, ½ teaspoon of cinnamon, ½ teaspoon of ground cumin, and ½ teaspoon of ground cardamom.

Chickpea and Winter Squash Tagine

SERVES 4 TO 6 ◆ PREP TIME: 15 minutes ◆ **COOK TIME:** 15 minutes

Tagine refers to a cooking vessel, an earthenware pot with a low, flat base and a tall triangular lid. Tagines vary in size and are often elaborately decorated. They are designed to cook slowly over low heat or coals. The conical lid seals tightly, creating a space for the food to steam. Tagine is also the name for the dish made in the vessel, usually meat or vegetables which are typically served with only a rice side dish to complete the meal. This tagine features butternut squash to minimize prep time, because it's often available prepped and precut in grocery stores. Raisins and vinegar create a lovely sweet-sour flavor that can be enhanced with a drizzle of Tahini Sauce (page 118).

¼ cup extra-virgin olive oil

1 onion, diced

1 garlic clove, minced

2 celery stalks, diced

2 teaspoons Baharat (page 121)

Pinch red pepper flakes

1 (15-ounce) can chickpeas, drained and rinsed

2 cups cubed butternut squash (about ½-inch)

6 cups vegetable broth or water

1 (8-ounce) can tomato sauce

1 teaspoon kosher salt

¼ teaspoon freshly ground black pepper

¼ cup packed raisins

¼ cup chopped fresh cilantro

1 tablespoon red wine vinegar

1. In a large pot over high heat, warm the olive oil. Add the onion, garlic, and celery and sauté until softened, 3 to 5 minutes. Add the baharat and red pepper flakes and sauté until aromatic, about 30 seconds.

2. Add the chickpeas, squash, broth, tomato sauce, salt, and pepper and bring to a boil. Reduce the heat to low and simmer to develop the flavors, 5 to 8 minutes.

3. Add the raisins and simmer for 1 minute to plump.

4. Turn off the heat, add the cilantro and vinegar, and mix well.

5. Ladle the tagine into bowls and serve.

Did You Know? Chickpeas were among the first beans to be cultivated and are believed to have originated in the Middle East. You can eat them fresh when green, as well as cooked, dried, or ground into a flour that can be used to make falafel or savory pancakes.

Chicken and Apricot Tagine,
page 67

Chapter 5

POULTRY, BEEF, AND LAMB

Chicken "Kebabs"

SERVES 4 TO 6 ♦ **PREP TIME:** 15 minutes ♦ **COOK TIME:** 15 minutes

Skewered, grilled meat is a traditional preparation in many Middle Eastern countries. This recipe is not a kebab, because the chicken isn't threaded on a skewer to save time, but you can take this step if you desire. The yogurt in the recipe is seasoned with classic Middle Eastern spices cumin, cinnamon, and red pepper flakes, and it tenderizes the chicken while adding moisture. The seasoned chicken pieces are baked in a hot oven, cooking quickly, to achieve the kebab taste in less time. Serve with Roasted Vegetables with Baharat (page 45) and naan or pita bread.

1 cup plain whole-milk Greek yogurt

3 tablespoons extra-virgin olive oil, divided

1 garlic clove, minced

½ teaspoon ground cumin

½ teaspoon ground cinnamon

Pinch red pepper flakes

1 teaspoon kosher salt

¼ teaspoon freshly ground black pepper

2 pounds boneless, skinless chicken thighs, cut into 2-inch pieces

¼ cup chopped fresh cilantro

1. Preheat the oven to 400°F.

2. In a large bowl, whisk the yogurt, 2 tablespoons of olive oil, garlic, cumin, cinnamon, red pepper flakes, salt, and pepper until smooth.

3. Add the chicken and evenly coat it with the yogurt marinade.

4. Spread the remaining 1 tablespoon of olive oil evenly on a baking sheet.

5. Spread the chicken on the baking sheet in a single layer and roast until cooked through and browned, about 15 minutes.

6. Arrange the chicken on a serving platter, garnish with the cilantro, and serve.

Storage Tip: If time allows, marinate the chicken in the yogurt mixture overnight. Refrigerate any leftovers in an airtight container for up to 5 days; this dish doesn't freeze well.

Chicken and Apricot Tagine

SERVES 4 TO 6 ◆ **PREP TIME:** 10 minutes ◆ **COOK TIME:** 20 minutes

Combining meat and fruit is a hallmark of Moroccan cuisine. Fruit is also very compatible with Morocco's favored spices cinnamon, paprika, and turmeric. You can make this using fresh apricots when they are in season (use an equal amount of fresh), but it's easy to prepare year-round using dried. This tagine is best served with Harissa Paste (page 122) and rice.

¼ cup extra-virgin olive oil

1 onion, diced

1 garlic clove, minced

2 celery stalks, diced

1 teaspoon ground cumin

1 teaspoon ground cinnamon

1 teaspoon smoked paprika

½ teaspoon ground turmeric

1½ pounds boneless, skinless chicken thighs, cut into 2-inch pieces

6 cups chicken broth or water

1 (15-ounce) can chickpeas, drained and rinsed

1 cup dried apricots, quartered

1 teaspoon kosher salt

¼ teaspoon freshly ground black pepper

¼ cup chopped fresh cilantro

1 tablespoon freshly squeezed lemon juice

1. In a large pot over medium-high heat, warm the olive oil. Add the onion, garlic, and celery and sauté until softened, 3 to 5 minutes. Add the cumin, cinnamon, paprika, and turmeric and sauté until aromatic, about 30 seconds.

2. Add the chicken and sauté to brown on all sides, about 5 minutes. Add the broth, chickpeas, apricots, salt, and pepper and bring to a boil.

3. Reduce the heat to low and simmer to develop the flavors and to thoroughly cook the chicken, 5 to 8 minutes.

4. Turn the heat off, add the cilantro and lemon juice, and mix well. Ladle the tagine into bowls and serve.

Substitution Tip: You can substitute 2 teaspoons of Baharat for the spices listed in the recipe. You can also add cauliflower florets and garnish with fresh mint.

Chicken in Pomegranate-Walnut Sauce

SERVES 4 TO 6 ♦ **PREP TIME:** 15 minutes ♦ **COOK TIME:** 15 minutes

This is a classic dish from Iran known as fesenjan. The chicken is browned in butter and simmered with onions, chicken broth, and pomegranate molasses and finished with a generous dusting of toasted walnuts and pomegranate arils. Add a dollop of yogurt to the dish for a creamy sauce. Serve with rice or bulgur and Persian Spiced Cauliflower (page 96) for a complete dinner.

1 cup chopped walnuts

2 tablespoons butter

2 pounds boneless, skinless chicken breasts or thighs, cut into 2-inch pieces

2 cups chicken broth or water

1 onion, diced

1 garlic clove, minced

½ teaspoon ground turmeric

¼ teaspoon ground cinnamon

¼ teaspoon ground nutmeg

¼ cup pomegranate molasses

1 teaspoon kosher salt

¼ teaspoon freshly ground black pepper

½ cup pomegranate arils

¼ cup chopped fresh parsley

1. In a large skillet over high heat, cook the walnuts until lightly browned, about 2 minutes. Remove the nuts from the skillet to a small bowl and set them aside.

2. Melt the butter in the same skillet and brown the chicken on all sides, 4 to 5 minutes.

3. Add the toasted walnuts, chicken broth, onion, garlic, turmeric, cinnamon, nutmeg, and pomegranate molasses and bring to a boil.

4. Reduce the heat to low, cover, and simmer until the chicken is cooked through, about 10 minutes.

5. Add the salt, pepper, pomegranate arils, and parsley and mix well. Transfer to a serving dish and serve hot.

Shawarma-Spiced Chicken

SERVES 4 TO 6 ♦ **PREP TIME:** 15 minutes ♦ **COOK TIME:** 15 minutes

Shawarma, an Arabic word, refers to seasoned meats stacked on a vertical spit. This dish is believed to have originated in Turkey but is enjoyed throughout the Middle East. As the meat cooks, it's sliced off in thin strips and served on flatbread with yogurt sauce. I've created a homemade version by roasting seasoned chicken in the oven and serving it with Toum and pita or naan.

¼ cup extra-virgin olive oil

2 tablespoons freshly squeezed lemon juice

1 teaspoon ground coriander

1 teaspoon ground cumin

1 teaspoon ground cardamom

1 teaspoon smoked paprika

1 teaspoon kosher salt

¼ teaspoon freshly ground black pepper

2 pounds boneless, skinless chicken thighs, cut into 2-inch pieces

4 to 6 pita breads

1 cup Toum (page 119)

1. Preheat the oven to 400°F.

2. In a large bowl, whisk the olive oil, lemon juice, coriander, cumin, cardamom, paprika, salt, and pepper to combine.

3. Add the chicken and mix to coat the chicken evenly with the spice mixture.

4. Place the chicken on a baking sheet and spread it out evenly.

5. Roast until the chicken is cooked through and lightly browned, about 15 minutes.

6. To serve, place several chicken pieces on each pita and divide the Toum between the pitas. Fold in half and serve.

Cooking Tip: If time allows, marinate the chicken in the spice mix overnight.

Substitution Tip: You can make a quick Toum by combining 1 cup of yogurt with ¼ teaspoon of garlic powder and a squeeze of lemon juice.

Squash Stuffed with Spiced Chicken and Chickpeas

SERVES 4 TO 6 ♦ **PREP TIME:** 15 minutes ♦ **COOK TIME:** 15 minutes

Delicata squash is the perfect vehicle for this mixture of chicken and chickpeas. There is no need to peel the squash if you wash them. This dish was inspired by the stuffed vegetables enjoyed throughout the Middle East and the Mediterranean. Typically, raw vegetables are stuffed with an uncooked meat mixture and cooked low and slow until tender. We save time by cooking the squash and filling separately and stuffing the squash boats with the meat mixture. I like to drizzle Tahini Sauce (page 118) over the stuffed squash and serve them with Beet Salad with Pomegranate Molasses and Pistachios (page 54).

4 tablespoons extra-virgin olive oil, divided

2 small to medium Delicata squash, washed, halved lengthwise, and seeded

1¼ teaspoons kosher salt, divided

½ pound ground chicken

1 (15-ounce) can chickpeas, drained and rinsed

½ cup chicken broth or water

1 teaspoon smoked paprika

½ teaspoon ground cinnamon

Pinch red pepper flakes

2 scallions, white and green parts, thickly sliced

½ cup chopped fresh cilantro

2 tablespoons toasted slivered almonds

1. Preheat the oven to 400°F. Spread 2 tablespoons of olive oil evenly on a baking sheet.

2. Season the squash with a ¼ teaspoon of salt and place them cut-side down on the baking sheet.

3. Roast until tender, 10 to 15 minutes.

4. While the squash is roasting, in a large skillet over high heat, warm the remaining 2 tablespoons of olive oil.

5. Add the chicken and break it up with a spoon and brown on all sides until no longer pink, about 5 minutes.

6. Add the chickpeas, the broth, the remaining 1 teaspoon of salt, the paprika, the cinnamon, and the red pepper flakes and bring to a simmer for 2 to 3 minutes, stirring frequently.

7. Add the scallions and cilantro and mix well.

8. When the squash is cooked, place each squash hollow-side up on a serving dish. Divide the chicken mixture between the squash. Garnish each squash with the almonds and serve.

Substitution Tip: If small Delicata squash are unavailable, use one large squash, cut in half lengthwise and remove the seeds. Cut each half in half widthwise to make four pieces. Continue with the recipe as written.

Storage Tip: Refrigerate in an airtight container for up to 5 days; this dish does not freeze well.

Saffron Chicken, Zucchini, and Rice

SERVES 4 TO 6 ♦ PREP TIME: 10 minutes ♦ **COOK TIME:** 20 minutes

This is a Middle Eastern version of chicken and rice. Saffron is the threads of the autumn crocus, or *Crocus sativus*, which is very difficult to harvest, making this spice very expensive. Its flavor is unique and impossible to replicate, but you can substitute turmeric to give this dish its classic gold-orange color.

2 tablespoons warm water

¼ teaspoon saffron or ground turmeric

2 tablespoons butter

1 tablespoon extra-virgin olive oil

1½ pounds boneless, skinless chicken thighs or breasts, cut into 2-inch pieces

1 onion, chopped

2 cups chicken broth

2 cups thinly sliced zucchini

1 cup basmati rice

¼ cup packed raisins or currants

1 teaspoon kosher salt

¼ teaspoon freshly ground black pepper

2 tablespoons chopped fresh parsley

1. In a small bowl, combine the warm water and saffron and set it aside for 5 minutes.

2. In a large skillet over high heat, warm the butter and olive oil. Once the butter melts, add the chicken and sauté until browned on all sides, about 5 minutes.

3. Add the onion, broth, zucchini, and rice and bring to a simmer.

4. Add the saffron mixture, raisins, salt, and pepper. Cover and simmer until the chicken is cooked through and the rice is tender, 10 to 15 minutes.

5. Transfer to a serving dish, garnish with the parsley, and serve.

Storage Tip: Refrigerate in an airtight container for up to 5 days; this recipe doesn't freeze well.

Kibbeh

MAKES 36 (1-OUNCE) MEATBALLS ♦ PREP TIME: 15 minutes ♦ COOK TIME: 15 minutes

Traditionally, kibbeh—the national dish of Syria—is a fried, oval-shaped stuffed meatball. The original recipe features an outer bulgur shell stuffed with a spice-scented meat and pine nut mixture. To make this a 30-minute dish, the bulgur and meat are combined and the round meatballs are baked. Serve these with Cucumber-Mint Yogurt Sauce (page 124) and Carrot Salad (page 53).

¼ cup extra-virgin olive oil

½ cup bulgur

1 cup boiling water

1 pound (85% lean) ground beef

1 onion, minced

½ cup toasted pine nuts

1 large egg

1 teaspoon ground allspice

1 teaspoon kosher salt

½ teaspoon freshly ground black pepper

¼ teaspoon ground cinnamon

1. Preheat the oven to 400°F. Grease a baking sheet with the olive oil.

2. In a large bowl, combine the bulgur and the boiling water. Cover and let it sit until tender and fluffy, 10 minutes. Drain and discard any additional water.

3. Add the ground beef, onion, pine nuts, egg, allspice, salt, pepper, and cinnamon and mix well.

4. Shape the meatballs into 36 (2-inch) meatballs and place them on the baking sheet, rotating them to coat with the olive oil.

5. Roast until the meatballs are cooked through, about 15 minutes.

6. Place the meatballs in a serving dish and serve hot.

Variation Tip: You can make a gluten-free version of these Kibbeh by substituting 2 cups of cooked millet for the bulgur.

Storage Tip: Refrigerate the cooked meatballs in an airtight container for up to 5 days, or freeze for 2 months.

Moroccan Spiced Chicken with Lemons and Olives

SERVES 4 TO 6 ♦ PREP TIME: 10 minutes ♦ **COOK TIME:** 20 minutes

This recipe calls for preserved lemons, a condiment used frequently throughout North Africa and India. Typically, lemons are preserved for weeks in a mixture of 2 parts salt and 1 part sugar. They are available in specialty markets and online. Preserved lemons are bitter and sweet, which complement the olives in this recipe. Serve this dish with couscous.

2 tablespoons extra-virgin olive oil

1½ pounds boneless, skinless chicken thighs or breasts, cut into 2-inch pieces

2 teaspoons paprika

1 teaspoon ground ginger

1 teaspoon ground turmeric

½ teaspoon ground cinnamon

1 teaspoon kosher salt

2 tablespoons butter

1 small red onion, chopped

2 garlic cloves, minced

1 cup pitted green olives

½ cup chicken broth or water

¼ cup chopped preserved lemon

¼ cup packed raisins or currants

¼ cup chopped fresh cilantro

¼ cup chopped fresh mint

1. In a large bowl, combine the oil and the chicken and toss to coat.

2. In a small bowl, combine the paprika, ginger, turmeric, cinnamon, and salt. Add the spices to the chicken and toss to coat.

3. In a large skillet over high heat, melt the butter.

4. Add the chicken and brown on all sides, about 5 minutes.

5. Add the onion, garlic, olives, broth, preserved lemon, and raisins and bring to a simmer.

6. Reduce the heat to low, cover, and simmer until the chicken has cooked through, 10 to 15 minutes.

7. Transfer to a serving dish, garnish with the cilantro and mint, and serve.

Substitution Tip: If you can't locate preserved lemons, substitute 1 tablespoon of lemon zest. Marinate the chicken overnight if possible.

Storage Tip: Refrigerate in an airtight container for up to 5 days; this recipe does not freeze well.

Did You Know? Citrus grows abundantly throughout the Middle East and Mediterranean, so preserving lemons, limes, and oranges is part of the cuisine. Preserved lemons are usually associated with Morocco, but Iran uses whole dried limes simmered in a stew or soup, crumbled in spice mixes, or as a finishing seasoning. Oranges are not indigenous to the Middle East, but they are cultivated there, and every good home cook has strips of orange peel hanging in their kitchen to throw into the stew pot.

Persian Beef Meatballs in Harissa Broth

SERVES 4 ◆ **PREP TIME:** 15 minutes ◆ **COOK TIME:** 15 minutes

This recipe is an excellent way to enjoy a meatball supper with some Middle Eastern flair. Giant meatballs are served in a broth that is enhanced with Harissa Paste and bulked up with potatoes. Cooking the meatballs in the oven speeds up the prep time, and simmering the potatoes in stock gives them extra flavor. Serve this dish with a simple salad and pita bread.

¼ cup extra-virgin olive oil

1 pound (85% lean) ground beef

1 onion, minced

2 garlic cloves, minced

1 large egg

¼ cup chopped fresh cilantro

¼ cup chopped fresh parsley

2 scallions, white and green parts, thinly sliced

1 teaspoon ground turmeric

1 teaspoon kosher salt

½ teaspoon freshly ground black pepper.

1 quart beef or chicken broth

2 cups peeled and cubed (1-inch) russet potatoes (about 5 medium)

4 parsley sprigs

¼ cup Harissa Paste (page 122)

1. Preheat the oven to 400°F. Grease a baking sheet with the olive oil.

2. In a large bowl, combine the ground beef, onion, garlic, egg, cilantro, parsley, scallions, turmeric, salt, and pepper and mix well.

3. Shape the mixture into 4 large meatballs.

4. Place the meatballs on the baking sheet and roast until cooked through, approximately 15 minutes.

5. While the meatballs are cooking, bring the broth to a boil, add the potatoes, and cook until tender, about 10 minutes.

6. To serve, place a meatball in each of four large soup bowls and spoon the potatoes and broth over each meatball. Garnish each bowl with a parsley sprig and harissa paste.

Substitution Tip: These meatballs are excellent with ground, lamb, or turkey. Add 4 cups of baby spinach to the broth to boost the vegetables. Substitute any hot sauce for the Harissa Paste.

Beef, Onion, and Noodle Stew

SERVES 4 TO 6 ♦ PREP TIME: 10 minutes ♦ **COOK TIME:** 20 minutes

Cubed beef simmered with cinnamon in tomato sauce is popular throughout the Middle East. Some countries include okra in this stew and serve it over rice; others add noodles to absorb all the delicious flavors. My version swaps in ground beef to shorten the cooking time. The noodles are cooked in the same pot with all the other ingredients, making this a one-pot meal.

½ cup extra-virgin
olive oil, divided

1 pound (85% lean)
ground beef

1 onion, minced

2 garlic cloves, minced

1 cup store-bought
tomato sauce

½ teaspoon ground
cinnamon

1 teaspoon kosher salt

½ teaspoon freshly
ground black pepper

4½ cups water

1 pound elbow macaroni

¼ cup plain whole-milk
Greek yogurt

¼ cup chopped
fresh parsley

1. In a large pot over high heat, warm ¼ cup of olive oil. Add the ground beef and brown the meat, using a large spoon to break it up, 5 to 8 minutes.

2. Add the onion and garlic and sauté until softened, about 3 minutes. Add the tomato sauce, cinnamon, salt, and pepper and mix well.

3. Add the water and macaroni and bring to a boil. Cover and cook until the pasta is tender, 8 to 10 minutes.

4. Turn off the heat and stir in the yogurt until well blended. Transfer to a serving dish and garnish with the parsley and the remaining ¼ cup of olive oil.

Substitution Tip: This dish can be made with ground lamb or turkey. For extra flavor, substitute marinara sauce for the tomato sauce. Any type of pasta will work in this recipe if you follow the cooking times suggested on the package.

Storage Tip: Refrigerate in an airtight container for up to 5 days, or freeze for 2 months.

Beef and Lamb Kofta

MAKES 8 KOFTA ♦ PREP TIME: 10 minutes ♦ **COOK TIME:** 15 minutes

Kofta refers to the meatballs favored throughout the Middle East. Kofta are typically finger-shaped, so they can be skewered and grilled—when on a skewer, they become kofta kebabs. I made them into balls in this recipe and baked them in a hot oven to save time.

¼ cup extra-virgin olive oil

1 pound (85% lean) ground beef

½ pound ground lamb

1 onion, minced

2 garlic cloves, minced

⅓ cup chopped fresh parsley

1 teaspoon kosher salt

½ teaspoon ground allspice

½ teaspoon ground cardamom

½ teaspoon sumac

½ teaspoon paprika

¼ teaspoon ground nutmeg

¼ teaspoon freshly ground black pepper

4 to 6 pita breads

½ cup Tahini Sauce (page 118)

1 cup chopped tomatoes

¼ cup chopped fresh parsley

1. Preheat the oven to 400°F. Grease a baking sheet with the olive oil.

2. In a large bowl, combine the ground beef, ground lamb, onion, garlic, parsley, salt, allspice, cardamom, sumac, paprika, nutmeg, and pepper and mix well.

3. Divide the meat mixture into 8 pieces and shape them into long, flat meatballs, about 3 to 4 inches long and 1 inch wide.

4. Place the meatballs on the baking sheet and roast until lightly browned and cooked through, about 15 minutes.

5. To serve, place the kofta on the pita breads and drizzle with tahini sauce. Garnish with tomatoes and parsley and fold in half to eat.

Cooking Tip: Pita bread is easier to use when warmed. To warm them up, wrap them in foil and place them in 400°F oven for 5 minutes. Remove from the oven and keep wrapped until ready to use.

Storage Tip: Refrigerate for up to 5 days, or freeze for 1 month.

Lamb Merguez

SERVES 4 ♦ **PREP TIME:** 10 minutes ♦ **COOK TIME:** 15 minutes

Merguez is a spicy garlic sausage typically made with lamb and stuffed in a casing. In this recipe, the mixture is shaped like a hamburger patty for quick cooking. Use a merguez patty to make a delicious Middle Eastern burger topped with lettuce, tomato, red onion, Pickled Vegetables (page 42), and Cucumber-Mint Yogurt Sauce (page 124).

2 tablespoons extra-virgin olive oil	2 tablespoons Harissa Paste (page 122)	½ teaspoon fennel seeds, crushed
1 pound ground lamb	1 tablespoon paprika	½ teaspoon ground cumin
2 garlic cloves, minced	1 teaspoon kosher salt	½ teaspoon ground coriander

1. Preheat the oven to 400°F. Grease a baking sheet with the olive oil.

2. In a large bowl, combine the ground lamb, garlic, harissa paste, paprika, salt, fennel seeds, cumin, and coriander and mix well.

3. Shape the mixture into 4 (½-inch thick) patties and place them on the baking sheet.

4. Roast until lightly browned and cooked through, about 15 minutes.

5. Serve the patties hot.

Make-Ahead Tip: If time allows, make the meat mixture 24 hours ahead to give the flavors time to meld.

Storage Tip: Refrigerate in an airtight container for 5 days, or freeze for 2 months.

Spiced Lamb and Vegetables with Rice

SERVES 4 TO 6 ♦ **PREP TIME:** 10 minutes ♦ **COOK TIME:** 20 minutes

This ground lamb dish is seasoned with cinnamon and turmeric and cooked with basmati rice and tomatoes for a one-pot meal. Fava beans are traditionally an early crop. Including them here creates a lovely springtime dish, even though this recipe uses frozen fava beans for easy prep.

¼ cup extra-virgin olive oil

1 pound ground lamb

1 garlic clove, minced

1 teaspoon ground turmeric

½ teaspoon ground cardamom

⅛ teaspoon ground cloves

1 cinnamon stick

1 teaspoon kosher salt

¼ teaspoon freshly ground black pepper

2 cups chicken broth or water

1 cup basmati rice

¼ cup packed raisins or currants

1 cup frozen fava beans

2 Roma tomatoes, chopped

2 scallions, white and green parts, thinly sliced

2 tablespoons chopped fresh cilantro

¼ cup toasted slivered almonds

1. In a large skillet over high heat, warm the oil. Add the ground lamb and brown, using a large spoon to break it up, about 5 minutes.

2. Add the garlic, turmeric, cardamom, cloves, cinnamon stick, salt, and pepper and mix well.

3. Add the broth, rice, and raisins and bring to a simmer. Add the fava beans and tomatoes. Cover, reduce the heat to low, and simmer until the rice is tender, about 15 minutes.

4. Transfer to a serving dish. Garnish with the scallions, cilantro, and almonds and serve.

Substitution Tip: This dish can be made with ground beef or turkey instead. If frozen fava beans aren't available, substitute frozen peas or lima beans.

Storage Tip: Refrigerate in an airtight container for up to 5 days, or freeze for 2 months.

Spiced Lamb and Pine Nut Pita Pizzas

SERVES 4 ♦ **PREP TIME:** 10 minutes ♦ **COOK TIME:** 20 minutes

Who doesn't love lamb seasoned with garlic, Za'atar, and tomatoes, spread on pita bread and topped with crumbled feta and Tahini Sauce? This flavorful mixture was stuffed originally into a pocket, but once the world discovered pizzas, the filling ended up on top. If time allows, grill the pita before adding the toppings to add a charred flavor. Other toppings can include thinly sliced cucumbers and pitted olives.

¼ cup extra-virgin olive oil

1 pound ground lamb

2 garlic cloves, minced

2 teaspoons Za'atar (page 120)

1 teaspoon kosher salt

¼ teaspoon freshly ground black pepper

2 Roma tomatoes, chopped

4 (6½-inch) pita breads

2 ounces crumbled feta

1 scallion, white and green parts, thinly sliced

2 tablespoons chopped fresh cilantro

½ cup Tahini Sauce (page 118)

1. Preheat the oven to 400°F.

2. Heat the oil in a large skillet over high heat. Add the ground lamb and brown, using a large spoon to break it up, about 5 minutes.

3. Add the garlic, za'atar, salt, and pepper and mix well. Add the tomatoes and cook to blend, about 5 minutes.

4. Place the pitas on a baking sheet. Divide the lamb between the pitas and top with the feta. Roast until the pizzas are lightly toasted, 5 to 8 minutes.

5. Place the pizzas on serving dishes and garnish with the scallion, cilantro, and tahini sauce.

Substitution Tip: Merguez is a great substitute for the spiced lamb in this dish.

Storage Tip: Refrigerate the lamb mixture in an airtight container for up to 5 days, or freeze for 2 months.

Grilled Onion and Sumac Lamb Chops

SERVES 4 ♦ PREP TIME: 15 minutes ♦ **COOK TIME:** 10 minutes

This is one of my Middle Eastern–ish recipes, using classic ingredients in new ways. Lamb loin chops are marinated in an onion-sumac mixture and grilled. If sumac isn't available, substitute the zest and juice of 1 lemon in the marinade. If time allows, the chops can marinate overnight. Serve with Israeli Couscous Salad (page 38).

¼ cup extra-virgin olive oil

2 tablespoons red wine vinegar

1 small yellow onion, coarsely chopped

1 teaspoon sumac

1 garlic clove

1 teaspoon smoked paprika

1 teaspoon salt

¼ teaspoon freshly ground black pepper

8 lamb loin chops

1. In the bowl of a blender or food processor, place the olive oil, vinegar, onion, sumac, garlic, paprika, salt, and pepper and blend until smooth. Add a little water as needed to achieve a loose texture.

2. Place the lamb chops in a shallow dish and pour the marinade over. Marinate for at least 15 minutes, or longer if time allows.

3. Heat a grill pan over high heat until very hot.

4. Remove the chops from the marinade, wiping off any excess marinade to prevent burning.

5. Place the chops on the grill and cook until seared with good grill marks, 3 to 4 minutes. Turn the chops and cook for an additional 3 to 4 minutes. Do not overcrowd the pan. Let the chops rest for 5 minutes before serving.

Variation Tip: You can also make this dish in a skillet if you don't own a grill pan—a cast-iron one works best for getting the same sear on the chop. Just use the same method described above.

Mussels and Squid with Couscous,
page 102

Chapter 6

SEAFOOD AND VEGETARIAN

Falafel

MAKES ABOUT 10 FALAFEL ♦ PREP TIME: 15 minutes ♦ **COOK TIME:** 15 minutes

The best falafel I ever ate was on Telegraph Avenue, outside the UC Berkeley campus, at a family-owned falafel stand. Their delicious stuffed pita sandwiches were so loaded with toppings they were almost impossible to eat. Authentic falafel are made with dried chickpeas that are soaked overnight, finely chopped, and mixed with spices and herbs. The mixture sits for several hours before it is shaped and deep-fried. In this recipe, chickpea flour and panfrying the falafel save time. This version is more a batter than a dough, so the finished product is a patty rather than a ball. Serve this falafel with tahini or Tahini Sauce and Cabbage with Herbed Citrus Yogurt (page 55).

1 cup chickpea flour

½ teaspoon kosher salt

¼ teaspoon baking soda

½ teaspoon ground cumin

½ teaspoon garlic powder

½ teaspoon onion powder

Pinch red pepper flakes

½ cup hot water

1 tablespoon freshly squeezed lemon juice

1 tablespoon chopped fresh parsley

¼ cup extra-virgin olive oil

1 cup Tahini Sauce (page 118) or tahini

OPTIONAL GARNISHES

Chopped romaine lettuce

Chopped tomatoes

Chopped fresh parsley

Chopped fresh cilantro

Cucumber-Mint Yogurt Sauce (page 124)

Harissa Paste (page 122)

Pita bread, for serving

1. In a large bowl, combine the chickpea flour, salt, baking soda, cumin, garlic powder, onion powder, and red pepper flakes. Mix well.

2. Add the hot water and lemon juice and mix thoroughly. Add the parsley and mix well. Let the batter rest for 10 minutes, or longer if time allows.

3. Place a large skillet over high heat, add the olive oil, and reduce the heat to medium-high.

4. Drop the batter into the oil by tablespoons once the oil is hot. Do not overcrowd the pan, and cook in batches if necessary.

5. Cook the falafel until golden on one side, 2 to 3 minutes. Flip and brown the other side for another 2 to 3 minutes.

6. Place the cooked falafel to drain on a plate lined with paper towels, and repeat with the remaining batter if necessary.

7. Arrange the falafel on a platter and serve warm with tahini sauce and any optional garnishes of your choice.

Ingredient Tip: Chickpea flour is available at most gourmet markets, health food stores, and online. There is no substitute for it.

Storage Tip: Refrigerate the falafel in an airtight container for up to 1 week, or freeze for several months.

Yogurt-Roasted Cauliflower with Harissa and Herbs

SERVES 4 TO 6 ♦ **PREP TIME:** 10 minutes ♦ **COOK TIME:** 20 minutes

This recipe is what I call a Middle Eastern-ish dish. A head of cauliflower is cut into 1-inch steaks, marinated in a saffron-yogurt sauce, and roasted. Cauliflower is a wonderfully versatile vegetable that lends itself to many applications. This is a riff on the classic whole roasted cauliflower; slicing it into steaks shortens the cooking time and makes it easier to eat. Serve with additional yogurt sauce, Harissa Paste, and a shower of herbs.

2 tablespoons extra-virgin olive oil, divided

1 large head cauliflower, cut into 1-inch slices

½ teaspoon kosher salt

¼ teaspoon freshly ground black pepper

2 tablespoons warm water

Pinch saffron

2 cups plain whole-milk Greek yogurt

1 garlic clove, minced

1 tablespoon grated lemon zest

1 tablespoon honey

¼ cup Harissa Paste (see page 122) or other hot sauce

¼ cup chopped fresh cilantro

1 tablespoon chopped fresh parsley

1. Preheat the oven to 400°F. Brush a baking sheet with 1 tablespoon of olive oil.

2. Lay the cauliflower slices on the baking sheet in a single layer. Brush the slices with the remaining 1 tablespoon of olive oil and season with the salt and pepper. Roast for 10 minutes.

3. While the cauliflower roasts, in a small bowl, combine the warm water and saffron until the saffron blooms, about 3 minutes.

4. In a small bowl, whisk the yogurt, garlic, lemon zest, honey, and saffron water until smooth.

5. Remove the cauliflower from the oven, brush each slice with the yogurt sauce, and return to the oven. Bake until the cauliflower is tender, 5 to 10 minutes.

6. Arrange the cauliflower on a serving dish and garnish it with any remaining yogurt sauce, harissa paste, cilantro, and parsley.

7. Serve hot or at room temperature.

Substitution Tip: You can substitute Toum (page 119) for the yogurt sauce.

Storage Tip: Refrigerate the cauliflower for up to 5 days; this dish does not freeze well.

Tomatoes Stuffed with Lentil Salad

SERVES 4 TO 6 ◆ PREP TIME: 10 minutes

Stuffed vegetables are served throughout the Middle East and are often filled with ground meat, grains, and beans. This is a way to use up a bumper crop of tomatoes, peppers, or cucumbers by turning them into filling main dishes. This recipe uses canned lentils, which makes this an anytime recipe. This is a mildly seasoned dish; you can punch up the seasoning by adding 1 teaspoon of Za'atar (page 120) to the filling or by serving topped with Tahini Sauce (page 118). To make a complete meal, serve these stuffed tomatoes with Tabbouleh (page 44).

1 (15-ounce) can lentils, drained and rinsed

¼ cup extra-virgin olive oil

1 tablespoon red wine vinegar

2 celery stalks, chopped

1 garlic clove, minced

2 scallions, white and green parts, thinly sliced

2 tablespoons chopped fresh parsley

2 tablespoons chopped fresh mint

½ teaspoon kosher salt

¼ teaspoon freshly ground black pepper

4 to 6 medium tomatoes, ripe but firm

1. In a large bowl, combine the lentils, olive oil, red wine vinegar, celery, garlic, scallions, parsley, mint, salt, and pepper. Mix well.

2. Cut the top third off of each tomato and scoop out the seeds, being careful not to break the shell.

3. Place the tomatoes on a serving dish and divide the lentil mixture between the tomatoes.

4. Replace the tops, if desired, and serve.

Substitution Tip: Try adding feta cheese to the lentil mixture. Once the lentil salad is added to the tomatoes, it's best to eat them within 24 hours. The lentil mixture can be refrigerated for up to 5 days. This recipe cannot be frozen.

Did You Know? Tomatoes, originally from South America, were first grown in Aleppo in the late 1700s and quickly became a popular fruit because they were easy to cultivate. They were initially only eaten cooked in a stew or sauce. Eating them raw came later.

Eggplant with Baked Eggs

SERVES 4 ♦ PREP TIME: 10 minutes ♦ **COOK TIME:** 15 minutes

Eggplant is a mainstay vegetable used throughout the Middle East and Mediterranean. This dish is an eggplant shakshuka, although you can substitute zucchini for the eggplant. If time allows, you can make the eggplant mixture ahead and reheat it before adding the eggs to finish the dish. Add crumbled feta or olives and serve with pita or naan bread for a complete meal; you can also omit the eggs and serve this as a side dish with roast lamb or beef.

¼ cup extra-virgin olive oil

1 large eggplant, cut into 1-inch cubes

1 teaspoon kosher salt

¼ teaspoon freshly ground black pepper

1 small red onion, chopped

1 garlic clove, sliced

2 teaspoons sweet paprika

1 teaspoon ground cumin

Pinch red pepper flakes

1 cup crushed tomatoes

½ cup water

4 large eggs

2 tablespoons chopped fresh cilantro

1. In a large skillet over high heat, warm the oil. Add the eggplant, salt, and pepper and sauté to brown the eggplant, about 5 minutes.

2. Add the onion, garlic, paprika, cumin, and red pepper flakes and mix well. Add the crushed tomatoes and water and bring to a simmer.

3. Reduce the heat to low, cover, and simmer until the eggplant is soft, about 5 minutes. Use a large spoon to mash the sauce coarsely.

4. Use the back of the spoon to create four evenly spaced wells in the sauce and carefully crack 1 egg into each one of the wells.

5. Reduce the heat to medium, cover, and cook until the eggs firm, 4 to 5 minutes.

6. Garnish with the cilantro and serve.

Substitution Tip: Make this dish vegan by omitting the eggs and adding 1 (15-ounce) can of beans of your choice, drained. The sauce (sans eggs) can be refrigerated for up to 1 week or frozen for several months.

Egyptian Moussaka

SERVES 4 ♦ **PREP TIME:** 10 minutes ♦ **COOK TIME:** 20 minutes

There are classic dishes prepared throughout the Middle East, and moussaka is one. The country of origin is up for debate. The moussaka we are most familiar with—layers of eggplant, meat, and béchamel sauce—is thought to have been created by a Greek chef around 1920. This version, taught to me by an Egyptian chef, was a revelation. It uses both canned tomato sauce and roasted peppers, the sweetness of which bring out the best flavors of the eggplant.

1 eggplant, cut into ½-inch slices

3 tablespoons extra-virgin olive oil, divided

½ teaspoon kosher salt

2 cups store-bought tomato sauce with garlic

2 ounces roasted red peppers, thinly sliced

1 tablespoon fresh oregano leaves

¼ teaspoon red pepper flakes (optional)

1. Preheat the oven to 400°F.

2. Place the eggplant on a baking sheet. Brush the slices on both sides with 2 tablespoons of olive oil and season with the salt.

3. Roast until the eggplant is cooked through, approximately 10 minutes.

4. Remove from the oven, and transfer the eggplant to a 9-by-13-inch oven-safe baking dish. Evenly spoon the tomato sauce over the eggplant, top with the roasted red peppers, and return to the oven to heat through, about 10 minutes.

5. Remove the dish from the oven. Garnish with the oregano leaves, drizzle with the remaining 1 tablespoon of olive oil, and sprinkle with the red pepper flakes (if using).

Substitution Tip: Use any tomato sauce or pasta sauce that you like. Freeze any unused sauce for another use.

Chickpea Cakes

MAKES 6 TO 8 CAKES ♦ **PREP TIME:** 15 minutes ♦ **COOK TIME:** 15 minutes

Similar to Falafel (page 86), these patties are more toothsome and a bit homier. They are made with bulgur, tahini, and chickpeas, rather like a Middle Eastern–inspired bean burger. I enjoy them simply, hot out of the oven with a squeeze of lemon and a dollop of Muhammara (page 43). Another way to enjoy them is to serve them with Pickled Vegetables (page 42) and Roasted Vegetables with Baharat (page 45). Serve leftovers crumbled over Fattoush (page 52).

1 cup bulgur

1½ cups boiling water

1 (15-ounce) can chickpeas, drained and rinsed

2 scallions, white and green parts, chopped

2 garlic cloves, sliced

¼ cup tahini

½ cup all-purpose flour or chickpea flour

¼ cup chopped fresh parsley

1 teaspoon kosher salt

¼ teaspoon freshly ground black pepper

4 tablespoons extra-virgin olive oil

1. Preheat the oven to 400°F.

2. In a large bowl, combine the bulgur and the boiling water. Cover and let sit until tender and fluffy, 10 to 15 minutes. Drain any excess water.

3. Place the chickpeas, scallions, garlic, and tahini in a food processor and pulse until the mixture is finely chopped but still has texture.

4. Add the chickpea mixture to the bulgur, then add the flour, parsley, salt, and pepper and mix well. The mixture will be sticky.

5. Grease a baking sheet with 2 tablespoons of olive oil.

6. Scoop the mixture into 2- to 3-ounce portions onto the baking sheet. Use an oiled spatula to flatten the mounds into patties about 2 inches in diameter. Once all the patties have been shaped, brush them with the remaining 2 tablespoons of olive oil.

7. Roast until cooked through, about 15 minutes.

8. Place on a serving dish and serve hot.

Cooking Tip: If time allows, the mixture will be easier to shape if it rests for 30 minutes.

Storage Tip: Refrigerate the patties for up to 5 days, or freeze for several months.

Persian Spiced Cauliflower

SERVES 4 ♦ **PREP TIME:** 10 minutes ♦ **COOK TIME:** 15 minutes

Advieh Spice Blend is a favored spice blend from Iran that can include exotic ingredients like dried limes and rose petals. My blend is made from easy-to-find ingredients. You're not limited to cauliflower; this spice blend works well on carrots, winter squashes, and beets, as well as fish and poultry. As is the custom in the Middle East, this dish can be served on a bed of yogurt with a drizzle of olive oil and a shower of herbs.

1 head cauliflower, cut into florets

¼ cup extra-virgin olive oil

1 tablespoon Advieh Spice Blend (page 123)

1 teaspoon sugar

½ teaspoon kosher salt

¼ teaspoon freshly ground black pepper

¼ cup chopped fresh cilantro (optional)

1. Preheat the oven to 400°F.

2. Place the cauliflower in a large bowl.

3. In a small bowl, whisk the olive oil, advieh, sugar, salt, and pepper until blended.

4. Pour the oil mixture over the cauliflower and toss to coat evenly.

5. Spread the cauliflower in a single layer on a baking sheet and roast until the cauliflower is tender and lightly browned, 10 to 15 minutes. If the cauliflower browns before cooking through, cover it with foil and roast until tender.

6. Place it on a serving dish, garnish with cilantro (if using), and serve hot or at room temperature.

Ingredient Tip: Advieh Spice Blend can be purchased online or at a good spice shop.

Whole Roasted Spiced Fish

SERVES 4 TO 6 ♦ **PREP TIME:** 10 minutes ♦ **COOK TIME:** 15 minutes

Whole roasted fish is easy, impressive, and flavorful, and most fish counters will clean a whole fish for you to make the job easier. It's best to order whole, cleaned fish ahead of time—just let the fishmonger know you plan to roast it whole. I use trout in this recipe because it's easy to find; it is on the smaller side and cooks quickly, and I suggest one trout per person. Serve this fish with Muhammara (page 43) and Cabbage with Herbed Citrus Yogurt (page 55).

4 tablespoons extra-virgin olive oil, divided

4 whole trout, cleaned and deboned

1 teaspoon Advieh Spice Blend (page 123)

½ teaspoon kosher salt

1 small lemon, thinly sliced

1 bunch thyme

4 scallions, white and green parts, chopped

1. Preheat the oven to 400°F. Brush a baking sheet with 1 tablespoon of olive oil, and arrange the trout on the baking sheet.

2. Brush the trout with the remaining 3 tablespoons of olive oil, making sure to brush the cavities as well. Season the fish inside and out with the advieh and salt.

3. Divide the lemon slices, thyme, and scallions between the fish, tucking them into the cavities.

4. Roast until the fish is cooked through and tender and the skin crispy, about 15 minutes.

Cooking Tip: If using a larger fish, the cooking time will increase.

Storage Tip: Refrigerate for up to 2 days; do not freeze this recipe.

Lentil, Brown Rice, and Caramelized Onion Stew

SERVES 4 TO 6 ◆ PREP TIME: 10 minutes ◆ **COOK TIME:** 15 minutes

This dish is inspired by kushari, a popular Egyptian street food with a base of lentils, rice, noodles, and caramelized onions that is topped with a spicy, tangy tomato sauce. I've omitted the noodles to simplify the recipe and use cooked rice and canned lentils. Cooked rice is available either frozen or in pouches in the international aisle; both are fine and can be reheated in the microwave. I use brown rice in this recipe, but any rice will do. Serve this dish with sautéed spinach for a complete meal.

2 tablespoons extra-virgin olive oil

1 onion, thinly sliced

2 garlic cloves, thinly sliced

2 cups cooked brown rice, heated according to package instructions

1 (15-ounce) can lentils, drained and rinsed

½ cup vegetable broth or water

1 teaspoon ground cumin

1 teaspoon kosher salt

¼ teaspoon freshly ground black pepper

¼ cup chopped fresh cilantro

3 scallions, white and green parts, sliced

OPTIONAL GARNISHES

1 cup plain whole-milk Greek yogurt

¼ cup Harissa Paste (page 122)

1. In a large skillet over high heat, warm the olive oil.

2. Once the oil is hot, add the onion and garlic, reduce the heat to medium-high, and cook, stirring frequently until the onion is golden brown, about 5 minutes. Remove the vegetables from the skillet and set them aside on a plate.

3. In the same skillet, combine the rice, lentils, broth, cumin, salt, and pepper. Mix well, cover, and cook over low heat until the mixture is heated through, 5 to 8 minutes.

4. Add the cilantro and scallions and mix well.

5. Transfer to a serving dish, spoon the onions over the rice, and serve alongside any optional garnishes.

Variation Tip: This dish is often served with crispy onions. To make crispy onions, increase the olive oil to ½ cup. Once hot, add the onions and fry over high heat until golden and crispy, then drain them on paper towels. The onions will go from golden to burnt in a matter of seconds, so don't walk away.

Storage Tip: Refrigerate this dish for up to 1 week, or freeze for several months.

Sheet Pan Salmon with Za'atar-Spiced Vegetables

SERVES 4 ♦ **PREP TIME:** 10 minutes ♦ **COOK TIME:** 20 minutes

Salmon is not native to the waters of the Middle East but is increasingly being farmed to meet customer demand. If you can find it where you are, wild salmon is always preferable. Be creative with your vegetables for this sheet pan supper—here, I use Delicata squash and red onions, but you can change it up seasonally. Za'atar is enjoying popularity right now, so it should be easy to find if you don't want to make your own. Add Lentil, Brown Rice, and Caramelized Onion Stew (page 98) for a complete meal.

6 tablespoons extra-virgin olive oil, divided

1 large Delicata squash, washed, seeded, and cut into ½-inch half-moons

1 red onion, thinly sliced

2 teaspoons Za'atar (page 120)

1½ pounds skin-on salmon fillet, cut into 4 portions

½ teaspoon kosher salt

¼ teaspoon freshly ground black pepper

¼ cup pistachios, chopped

¼ cup chopped fresh parsley

Grated zest of 1 lemon

1. Preheat the oven to 400°F.

2. Pour 4 tablespoons of olive oil onto a rimmed baking sheet. Add the Delicata squash and red onion and mix to coat the vegetables with the oil. Add the za'atar and mix to coat the vegetables evenly with the spice mixture.

3. Roast for 8 to 10 minutes. Remove from the oven and lay the salmon on top of the vegetables.

4. Season with the salt and pepper and roast until the salmon is cooked through, 15 to 20 minutes.

5. While the salmon is cooking, in a small bowl, combine the pistachios, parsley, the remaining 2 tablespoons of olive oil, and the lemon zest.

6. Arrange the vegetables on a serving platter and place the salmon on top of the vegetables. Spoon the pistachio sauce over the salmon and serve hot.

Substitution Tip: If pistachios aren't available, substitute almonds. Any firm-fleshed fish can be used instead of the salmon.

Storage Tip: Refrigerate in an airtight container for up to 2 days; do not freeze this dish.

Did You Know? Until recently, sardines, mackerel, and tuna were the most commonly eaten fish in the Middle East. Because of exposure to Western diets, the variety of seafood available has increased, with much of it coming from Egypt.

Mussels and Squid with Couscous

SERVES 4 TO 6 ♦ **PREP TIME:** 10 minutes ♦ **COOK TIME:** 20 minutes

Think of this as a paella with couscous. Any kind of fish or shellfish can be used, or you can substitute beans for the fish for a vegan version. Frozen precooked mussels and cleaned squid can be found in the seafood department in most stores—just thaw in the refrigerator overnight before using in this recipe. If you can't find frozen squid, ask your fishmonger to clean fresh squid for you. Muhammara (page 43) is my favorite accompaniment to this dish.

2 tablespoons extra-virgin olive oil

2 medium red peppers, stem and seeds removed, cut into ¼-inch dice

2 garlic cloves, peeled and sliced

1 tablespoon tomato paste

2 teaspoons smoked paprika

⅛ teaspoon red pepper flakes

¼ teaspoon saffron threads or ground turmeric

1 teaspoon salt

2 cups Israeli or pearl couscous

2½ cups broth or water

½ pound squid, cleaned and sliced into rings

½ pound cooked mussels, out of the shell

3 scallions, white and green part, thinly sliced

¼ cup chopped fresh Italian parsley

1. In a large frying pan or Dutch oven over high heat, warm the olive oil.

2. Add the red bell peppers and garlic and sauté until softened, about 2 minutes.

3. Add the tomato paste, paprika, and red pepper flakes and sauté until aromatic, about 30 seconds.

4. Add the saffron, salt, and couscous and sauté to mix well and slightly toast the couscous, about 2 minutes.

5. Add the broth and bring to a boil, then reduce the heat to simmer. Cover and cook until the couscous is tender, approximately 10 minutes.

6. Add the squid and mix well. Cover and cook over low heat until the squid has cooked through, 3 to 4 minutes.

7. Add the mussels and scallions and cook to warm the mussels through, about 2 minutes.

8. Top with the parsley and serve.

Did You Know?: This dish is best eaten the day it's made. Most markets sell squid or calamari that is battered and frozen; for this recipe, make sure you're buying a product that isn't seasoned or coated.

Variation: You can make this with regular couscous as well. Add peas for a pop of brightness.

Fish Pilaf

SERVES 4 TO 6 ♦ **PREP TIME:** 10 minutes ♦ **COOK TIME:** 20 minutes

This is a delicate dish of saffron basmati rice with roasted fish and slivered almonds. A firm-fleshed whitefish is ideal for this recipe. Saffron rice is eaten throughout the Middle East and India. When using saffron, it's always best to bloom it first in water or broth rather than adding the threads directly to the recipe, so the saffron disburses evenly. This is a dish that even seafood haters will enjoy. Serve it with Toum (page 119) and roasted vegetables for a complete meal.

2 tablespoons warm water

¼ teaspoon saffron or ground turmeric

2 tablespoons butter, divided

1 cup basmati rice

2 cups vegetable or chicken broth or water

1 teaspoon kosher salt

Pinch red pepper flakes

2 pounds firm whitefish fillet, cut into 2-inch pieces

¼ cup slivered almonds

Juice and grated zest of 1 lemon

2 scallions, white and green parts, thinly sliced

¼ cup chopped fresh parsley

1. In a small bowl, mix the water and saffron and set aside until the saffron blooms, about 5 minutes.

2. In a large skillet over high heat, melt 1 tablespoon of butter.

3. Add the rice and sauté to coat the rice with the butter, about 1 minute. Add the broth, saffron mixture, salt, and red pepper flakes and bring to a boil.

4. Reduce the heat to low, cover, and simmer to cook the rice partially, about 5 minutes.

5. Remove the lid and place the fish on top of the rice. Cover and continue to cook until the rice is tender and the fish is cooked through, 10 to 15 minutes.

6. While the fish cooks, melt the remaining 1 tablespoon of butter in a small skillet over medium heat.

7. Add the almonds and sauté until the almonds are lightly toasted.

8. Spoon the almonds and butter over the finished fish.

9. Add 2 tablespoons of lemon juice, 2 teaspoons of lemon zest, the scallions, and the parsley and serve.

Substitution Tip: Any long-grain white rice works well in this recipe. Trout and salmon can be used instead of whitefish.

Storage Tip: Refrigerate in an airtight container for up to 2 days; do not freeze this dish.

Rice Pudding,
page 109

Chapter 7

DESSERTS

Mamounia (Semolina Pudding)

SERVES 4 TO 6 ♦ PREP TIME: 10 minutes ♦ **COOK TIME:** 20 minutes

Considered a Syrian dish, this pudding has many versions throughout the Middle East and India. Typically, it's a mixture of toasted semolina, sugar syrup, nuts, and cinnamon, but other spices may be added depending on where it's being made. It is sometimes served with cheese and a drizzle of cream. This dish can be served as a dessert or breakfast porridge and is best enjoyed warm.

4 cups boiling water

1½ cups sugar

½ cup plus 1 tablespoon butter, divided

¼ cup pistachios, chopped

1 cup medium-grind semolina wheat

½ teaspoon ground cinnamon

1. In a medium bowl, whisk the boiling water and sugar until the sugar has dissolved and set it aside.

2. In a medium saucepan over high heat, melt 1 tablespoon of butter. Add the pistachios and sauté to toast the nuts lightly, about 3 minutes. Transfer the nuts to a plate and set them aside.

3. Melt the remaining ½ cup of butter in the saucepan over medium-high heat, add the semolina, and stirring constantly, cook until the semolina is toasted, 5 to 8 minutes.

4. Slowly add the sugar water to the semolina and bring to a boil. Reduce the heat to low and simmer, stirring constantly, until the mixture looks like thick cream, 2 to 4 minutes.

5. Pour the mixture into a serving dish, garnish with the pistachios and cinnamon, and serve.

Variation Tip: A gluten-free version can be made with millet, but the cooking time for that portion of the recipe will be significantly longer, about 20 minutes. Eat this pudding shortly after it's made; it will thicken as it cools.

Rice Pudding

SERVES 4 TO 6 ♦ **PREP TIME:** 10 minutes ♦ **COOK TIME:** 20 minutes

Every culture that eats rice has a version of rice pudding. In some recipes, the rice is slowly simmered in sweetened milk with a cinnamon stick; in others, cooked rice is added to vanilla custard. In some parts of the Middle East, rose water or orange blossom water and whole cloves are ingredients. This recipe is a combination of some of my favorite variations. To speed up cooking time, I start with cooked rice, either leftovers or precooked packaged rice. This can be served warm or eaten cold the next day.

2 cups cooked rice (reconstituted according to package directions, if needed)

2 to 3 cups whole milk

½ cup sugar

1 cinnamon stick

1 tablespoon grated orange zest

½ cup toasted slivered almonds (optional)

1. In a medium saucepan, combine the rice, milk, sugar, cinnamon stick, and orange zest.

2. Stirring constantly, bring to a simmer over medium-high heat. Still stirring, cook until the mixture is thick like porridge, 10 to 15 minutes. If it becomes too thick, add additional milk.

3. Remove from the heat and discard the cinnamon stick. Transfer the pudding to a serving dish, garnish with the almonds (if using), and serve.

Serving Tip: You can chill this pudding and eat it cold; just wait to add the almonds until you are ready to serve.

Storage Tip: Refrigerate for up to 1 week in an airtight container; do not freeze.

Did You Know? Although rice is a global crop, rice cultivation in the Middle East can be traced back to Iran as early as the first century CE. Rice spread throughout the Middle East and is grown in Egypt as a summer crop. Long-grain white rice or basmati rice has its origins in the foothills of the Himalayas.

Egyptian Milk Pudding

SERVES 4 TO 6 ♦ **PREP TIME:** 10 minutes ♦ **COOK TIME:** 15 minutes

Once you've had this pudding, you'll never want boxed stuff again. Traditionally, milk pudding is thickened with ground rice (or cream of rice cereal), but cornstarch is more reliable. It can be served warm or cold. If eaten warm, it's a delicious custard sauce. Try it poured over fresh fruit or Poached Pears in Orange Blossom Water (page 114). If you have time to chill it, garnish this pudding with fresh berries and a dusting of cinnamon sugar.

¾ cup sugar

2 tablespoons cornstarch

3 cups whole milk

2 teaspoons
   vanilla extract

½ teaspoon ground
   cinnamon (optional)

1. In a medium saucepan, whisk the sugar and cornstarch to combine.

2. Whisking the whole time, gradually add the milk.

3. Place the saucepan over high heat and cook, stirring constantly, until the mixture starts to boil.

4. Reduce the heat to low and simmer, stirring, until it is thickened, 5 to 10 minutes.

5. Turn off the heat, add the vanilla and cinnamon (if using), and mix well.

6. Pour into serving dishes and serve.

Variation Tip: To make the pudding extra rich, use 1 cup of heavy (whipping) cream and 2 cups of milk. If serving cold, chill for at least 2 hours.

Storage Tip: Refrigerate for up to 5 days; do not freeze.

Baklava Tartlets

MAKES 24 MINI TARTLETS ♦ PREP TIME: 15 minutes ♦ **COOK TIME:** 10 minutes

Phyllo is extraordinarily versatile, and you can shape it into anything. Typically, baklava is made of sheets of buttered phyllo layered with cinnamon sugar and nuts. We made it with walnuts and honey syrup in my family, but there are variations throughout the Middle East with pistachios or almonds and soaked in a rose or orange water syrup. For this recipe, I used premade fully cooked mini phyllo shells found in the grocery store's frozen section. These tartlets are fragile and should be eaten shortly after making them.

24 mini phyllo shells

6 ounces walnuts, finely chopped

½ cup honey

1 teaspoon ground cinnamon

2 teaspoons grated orange zest

1. Preheat the oven to 375°F.

2. Place the phyllo shells on a baking sheet or in a mini muffin tin (if they fit without wobbling).

3. In a small bowl, combine the walnuts, honey, cinnamon, and orange zest. Divide the walnut mixture between the tart shells.

4. Bake until the nut mixture begins to toast, 7 to 10 minutes. Do not overcook or the phyllo will burn.

5. Cool to room temperature and serve.

Substitution Tip: If you can't find phyllo shells, you can make them with a mini muffin tin and a pastry brush. Thaw frozen filo sheets overnight in the refrigerator, unwrap them, and lay them flat. Place one sheet on a work surface and brush it with melted butter or oil, top with another sheet, and brush again with melted butter or oil. Use a sharp knife to score into your desired size (2-inch squares for mini tarts). Invert and press the stacks buttered-side down into the mini muffin tin. Continue until the muffin tin is full. Follow the directions for the filling and bake for 10 to 15 minutes, or until the phyllo is golden.

Halvah

MAKES 24 PIECES ◆ **PREP TIME:** 10 minutes ◆ **COOK TIME:** 20 minutes

Halvah is a dense, fudgy confection made with sugar and tahini. There is also a Greek version that uses semolina instead of tahini, and adds nuts and dried fruits. This recipe is made with tahini and is very basic—what I refer to as Halvah 101. Once you've mastered this recipe, you can dress it up with nuts, spices, chocolate, other mix-ins, and flavors. A candy thermometer is helpful, but see the tip for how to make this without one.

2 cups sugar

½ cup water

1½ cups tahini

Pinch kosher salt

1 tablespoon vanilla extract

1. Line an 8-inch square baking pan with parchment paper.

2. In a medium saucepan over medium heat, combine the sugar and water, stirring frequently, until the sugar dissolves.

3. Bring to a boil, reduce the heat to low, and simmer with a candy thermometer lowered into the saucepan. Cook, stirring constantly, until the mixture reaches 245°F (soft ball stage).

4. Place the tahini and salt in the bowl of a stand mixer. With the machine running at medium speed, gradually add the sugar syrup.

5. Once all the syrup is added, beat in the vanilla. Halvah should have a fudge-like texture; it will harden as it cools.

6. Quickly transfer the mixture to the prepared pan, smooth, and set it aside to cool. Cut into 24 squares and serve.

Cooking Tip: To make halvah without a candy thermometer, drop a small spoonful of the sugar syrup into a bowl of tap water. If the syrup forms a ball that can be flattened, you're at the right temperature.

Storage Tip: Store in an airtight container at room temperature for up to 1 week.

Figs with Walnuts, Honey, and Yogurt

SERVES 4 ♦ PREP TIME: 10 minutes

This recipe is greater than the sum of its parts. Yogurt and honey are satisfying enough, but they become sublime when you add fresh figs. Greek yogurt is a must for this dessert; its thick, creamy texture and tanginess is the perfect partner for sweet figs. There is nothing better than figs when they are in season; however, if figs aren't available, then ripe plums are an excellent substitute.

2 cups plain whole-milk Greek yogurt

8 ripe figs, stemmed and quartered

8 tablespoons walnuts, coarsely chopped

½ cup honey

2 teaspoons chopped fresh mint

1. Divide the Greek yogurt between four small dishes.

2. Top each dish with 8 fig quarters and 2 tablespoons of walnuts.

3. Drizzle the dishes with honey, garnish with mint, and serve.

Substitution Tip: Almonds and pistachios are good substitutes for walnuts. It's important to use a full-flavored honey, like thyme or orange blossom. This dish should be eaten within an hour of assembling.

Did You Know? One way to be a successful 30-minute chef is to purchase chopped nuts, toast them, and store them in the freezer. To toast a large batch, line a small baking sheet with foil or parchment paper. Arrange the nuts in a single layer and bake in a 375°F oven until lightly golden brown, 5 to 6 minutes. If toasting a large batch of nuts, rotate the pan halfway through for even coloring. Cool the nuts completely. Use the corners of the parchment or foil to pick up the nuts and pour them into an airtight container or zip-top bag, and freeze them for up to 2 months.

Poached Pears in Orange Blossom Water

SERVES 4 ♦ PREP TIME: 15 minutes ♦ **COOK TIME:** 15 minutes

Since ancient times, quince has been a revered fruit throughout the Middle East and the Mediterranean. I remember being very puzzled by them when I first saw one, as it looked like a misshapen apple and smelled like a pear. In this recipe, we get inspiration from a classic Middle Eastern quince dish but instead use pears, which are easy to source and cook quickly. It's best to use pears that are a tad underripe. If, however, you find quince at the farmers' market or perhaps on a neighbor's tree, try them in this preparation but add 45 minutes to the cooking time.

½ cup honey

⅓ cup orange blossom water

1 vanilla bean, split

4 cups water

4 Bosc or Asian pears, peeled, cored, and quartered

1. In a medium saucepan over high heat, combine the honey, orange blossom water, vanilla bean, and water and bring to a boil.

2. Gently add the pears, reduce the heat to medium-low, and simmer until tender, about 6 minutes.

3. Cool the pears and store them in the poaching liquid. Serve the poached pears warm or cold over yogurt or ice cream.

Ingredient Tip: Orange blossom water can be found in gourmet markets, specialty stores, or online. However, you can replicate the flavor in this recipe by adding ⅓ cup of orange juice and 1 tablespoon of orange zest.

Did You Know? The apple known as the forbidden fruit in the Bible was most likely a quince. Quince is native to Iran and Turkey and is unpalatable if eaten raw—it needs a long simmer or roast to bring out its apple-like flavor.

Middle Eastern Shortbread Cookies

MAKES 24 COOKIES ♦ **PREP TIME:** 10 minutes ♦ **COOK TIME:** 15 minutes

Everyone loves butter cookies, whether they're called ghraybeh, kourabi-ethes, Russian tea cakes, or Mexican wedding cookies. The name ghraybeh is believed to originate in Turkey and loosely translates to "dry biscuit." Because butter wasn't widely available until the nineteenth century, these cookies are a relatively modern recipe. Often, ghraybeh are reserved for special occasions.

1 cup butter, at room temperature

1½ cups powdered sugar, divided

1 large egg yolk

2 teaspoons vanilla extract

2 cups all-purpose flour

Pinch kosher salt

1. Preheat the oven to 375°F. Line two baking sheets with parchment paper.

2. Place the butter and 1 cup of powdered sugar in a stand mixer bowl and beat until light, about 2 minutes. Add the egg yolk and vanilla and beat to combine.

3. Add the flour and salt and mix on low until all the flour is incorporated. Shape the dough into 1½-inch balls, or use a 1-ounce scoop to portion out the dough.

4. Place them on the baking trays and flatten each with the palm of your hand. Bake until lightly golden, 13 to 15 minutes. Remove them from the oven and cool for 5 minutes.

5. Place the remaining ½ cup of powdered sugar in a fine-mesh strainer and dust the tops of the cookies. Cool the cookies to room temperature before serving.

6. Store them in an airtight container for up to 10 days at room temperature.

Variation Tip: A pistachio pressed into each cookie before baking makes a nice garnish. These cookies can be frozen for several months, but they'll need another dusting of powdered sugar before serving.

Cucumber-Mint Yogurt Sauce, page 124

Chapter 8

SPICES AND STAPLES

Tahini Sauce

MAKES ABOUT 2 CUPS ♦ PREP TIME: 10 minutes

While cooking with an Egyptian chef, I learned her secret to delicious hummus—she created a tahini *sauce* that she added to her hummus instead of using plain tahini. This sauce is perfect for dipping pita and vegetables in or drizzling over roasted vegetables or grilled lamb chops. It's also a great flavor enhancer for savory recipes that use tahini as an ingredient. Since tahini separates, stir it well before using it in this recipe.

1 cup tahini

⅔ cup cold water

½ cup freshly squeezed lemon juice

2 garlic cloves, grated

1 teaspoon kosher salt

Extra-virgin olive oil, for topping (optional)

Red pepper flakes, for topping (optional)

1. In a medium bowl, combine the tahini, water, lemon juice, garlic, and salt. Stir until smooth. If the sauce is too thick, thin it with more cold water.

2. Place the sauce in a serving bowl and top with olive oil and red pepper flakes (if using).

Ingredient Tip: Tahini thickens when mixed with other ingredients; cold water is the best way to loosen the texture. Tahini can be bitter, so it's important to taste various brands and find one you like. If using a bitter brand, sweeten it with a little honey or maple syrup.

Toum

MAKES ABOUT 2 CUPS ♦ PREP TIME: 10 minutes

Traditional toum is a Lebanese sauce very similar to aïoli that is made with garlic, oil, and lemon juice. This recipe makes a special, creamier yogurt version also known as Labneh bi Toum. You can make it with regular labneh or Greek yogurt. Since labneh is tarter than Greek yogurt, you may want to add the lemon juice to taste depending on which yogurt you use.

2 cups plain whole-milk
Greek yogurt or labneh

2 garlic cloves, minced
or grated

Juice of 1 lemon

1 teaspoon kosher salt

OPTIONAL GARNISHES

Extra-virgin olive oil

Red pepper flakes

Grated lemon zest

Dried or fresh mint

1. In a medium bowl, combine the yogurt, garlic, lemon juice, and salt. Stir until blended.

2. Let sit for 15 minutes before serving.

3. Transfer to a serving bowl and garnish with optional garnishes.

Serving Tip: The flavor will improve if this sauce is made several hours ahead.

Storage Tip: Refrigerate in an airtight container for up to 1 week.

Za'atar

MAKES ABOUT ½ CUP ♦ **PREP TIME:** 10 minutes

Za'atar is an herb and spice blend that is fairly easy to find in the market, and it is also very easy to make. It's an ancient herb blend that is built upon dried oregano, and it was thought to have medicinal properties in the ancient world. This blend combines thyme, oregano, and toasted sesame seeds, but feel free to customize the mix according to your preferences. One of my favorite ways to use Za'atar is to warm naan bread, slather it with yogurt, and top it with a generous sprinkling of this blend.

1 tablespoon dried thyme

1 tablespoon dried oregano

1 tablespoon ground cumin

1 tablespoon ground coriander

1 tablespoon sumac

1 tablespoon toasted sesame seeds

1 teaspoon kosher salt

¼ teaspoon Aleppo pepper flakes or red pepper flakes (optional)

1. In a small bowl combine the thyme, oregano, cumin, coriander, sumac, sesame seeds, salt, and Aleppo pepper flakes (if using) and mix well.

2. Store in a jar at room temperature for up to 1 month.

Storage Tip: Za'atar can also be stored in the freezer for 2 months. It's wonderful on roasted or grilled meats and seafood.

Baharat

MAKES ABOUT ½ CUP ♦ PREP TIME: 10 minutes

Baharat is a classic North African spice blend that imparts the warm, aromatic, sweet, and savory flavors that are the hallmark of the region's tagines. Barahat is believed to come from the Arabic word for "spice." The ingredients can vary from region to region throughout the Middle East, North Africa, and India, but it is always a combination of paprika, sweet spices, and savory spices. In addition to enhancing stews and soups, use this blend to season root vegetables or chicken before roasting.

1½ tablespoons paprika

1 tablespoon
   ground cumin

2 teaspoons ground
   coriander

1 teaspoon kosher salt

1 teaspoon ground
   cinnamon

½ teaspoon ground cloves

½ teaspoon ground
   cardamom

½ teaspoon ground
   black pepper

¼ teaspoon
   ground nutmeg

In a small bowl, combine the paprika, cumin, coriander, salt, cinnamon, cloves, cardamom, pepper, and nutmeg and mix well.

Storage Tip: Store Baharat at room temperature for several months.

Did You Know? Into spices? There are two ways to make them even more flavorful. One is to freshly grind them just before using them; a small spice or coffee grinder is a good tool to have on hand for this. Another way is to lightly toast whole spices in a dry skillet over low heat until fragrant, about 60 seconds. Immediately remove the spices from the skillet to stop the cooking, cool to room temperature, and grind them. Spices should be stored in an airtight container away from heat and sunlight.

Harissa Paste

MAKES ABOUT 1½ CUPS ♦ PREP TIME: 10 minutes

Harissa is a mixture of dried chiles, spices, and olive oil ground into a paste. Think of it as the sriracha of the Middle East. Harissa is an Arabic word meaning "to pound." Any variety of red pepper works fine, so choose from guajillo, chiles de Arbol, chipotle chiles, or whatever is available in your area. The spiciness depends on your preference. You can mix Harissa Paste with yogurt or mayonnaise to make a delicious dipping sauce.

4 ounces dried
   chiles of choice

6 ounces roasted
   red peppers

3 garlic cloves, sliced

1 teaspoon
   smoked paprika

1 teaspoon
   ground caraway

1 teaspoon ground cumin

1 teaspoon kosher salt

¼ cup extra-virgin olive oil

1. In a medium bowl, combine the chiles and enough hot water to cover them by 2 inches. Cover the bowl and set it aside for 15 to 20 minutes to allow the chiles to soften.

2. Drain the water, reserving ½ cup.

3. Place the chiles, reserved water, roasted red peppers, garlic, paprika, caraway, cumin, and salt in a food processor or blender and process until finely chopped.

4. Add the olive oil and process until the mixture is well blended but still has texture.

Storage Tip: Refrigerate in an airtight container for up to 10 days.

Variation Tip: Lemon juice, preserved lemons, tomato paste, sun-dried tomatoes, dried oregano, and mint can all provide a unique twist to this sauce.

Advieh Spice Blend

MAKES ABOUT 1 OUNCE ♦ **PREP TIME:** 10 minutes

Advieh is an Iranian spice blend with the warming flavors of cinnamon and cloves. It can include rose petals and dried limes. Because those ingredients can be difficult to find, they are omitted from this version. There are varieties of advieh blends customized for poultry, vegetables, and meat, so if using store-bought, be sure the blend is best for your recipe needs. My recipe is a "universal" blend that is wonderful on chicken, lamb, cauliflower, root vegetables, and potatoes.

1 teaspoon ground cumin

1 teaspoon ground coriander

1 teaspoon ground turmeric

1 teaspoon kosher salt

½ teaspoon ground ginger

¼ teaspoon ground cardamom

⅛ teaspoon ground cinnamon

⅛ teaspoon ground cloves

Pinch red pepper flakes

Pinch freshly ground black pepper

1. In a small bowl, combine the cumin, coriander, turmeric, salt, ginger, cardamom, cinnamon, cloves, red pepper flakes, and pepper.

2. Store in a jar at room temperature.

Storage Tip: Store this spice blend at room temperature for several months.

Cucumber-Mint Yogurt Sauce

MAKES ABOUT 2 CUPS ♦ PREP TIME: 15 minutes

Called tzatziki in various parts of the Middle East and raita in India, this sauce is made with fresh or dried mint, toasted spices, and can use cucumber or not. This recipe features cucumbers, fresh mint, and scallions for a light, refreshing sauce that lightens up other ingredients and dishes. Use it as a dip for Pita Chips (page 125) or as a sauce to accompany roasted salmon.

2 cups plain whole-milk Greek yogurt

1 garlic clove, minced

1 small cucumber, peeled, seeded, and grated

2 scallions, white and green parts, thinly sliced

1 bunch mint, finely chopped

1 teaspoon kosher salt

Extra-virgin olive oil, for garnish (optional)

1. In a medium bowl, combine the yogurt, garlic, cucumber, scallions, mint, and salt. Mix until blended.

2. Garnish with olive oil (if using) and serve.

Cooking Tip: To get a thicker sauce, place the grated cucumber in a strainer and tap to drain the excess liquid.

Storage Tip: Refrigerate this sauce in an airtight container for up to 5 days.

Pita Chips

MAKES 24 CHIPS ◆ PREP TIME: 10 minutes ◆ **COOK TIME:** 15 minutes

Pita chips are found in most grocery stores, but store-bought versions can be over-seasoned and crumble easily. This simple recipe is made with olive oil and salt and crisped in the oven. These chips are addictive to eat on their own and are hearty enough to hold any dip.

3 tablespoons extra-virgin olive oil, divided

3 (6-inch) pita breads, cut into 8 wedges each

½ teaspoon kosher salt

1. Preheat the oven to 400°F. Brush a baking sheet with 1 tablespoon of olive oil.

2. Arrange the pita wedges in a single layer on the baking sheet. Drizzle the remaining 2 tablespoons of olive oil over the pita wedges and sprinkle them with the salt.

3. Bake until the chips are golden and crisp, 12 to 15 minutes.

4. Remove the chips from the oven and let them cool completely before eating.

Storage Tip: To keep these chips crispy, store them in an airtight container for up to 5 days. If they get soft, pop them into a 400°F oven for a few minutes to crisp them back up. For longer storage, they can be frozen for 1 month.

MEASUREMENT CONVERSIONS

Volume Equivalents (Liquid)

US STANDARD	US STANDARD (OUNCES)	METRIC (APPROX.)
2 tablespoons	1 fl. oz.	30 mL
¼ cup	2 fl. oz.	60 mL
½ cup	4 fl. oz.	120 mL
1 cup	8 fl. oz.	240 mL
1½ cups	12 fl. oz.	355 mL
2 cups or 1 pint	16 fl. oz.	475 mL
4 cups or 1 quart	32 fl. oz.	1 L
1 gallon	128 fl. oz.	4 L

Oven Temperatures

FAHRENHEIT (F)	CELSIUS (C) (APPROX.)
250°	120°
300°	150°
325°	165°
350°	180°
375°	190°
400°	200°
425°	220°
450°	230°

Volume Equivalents (Dry)

US STANDARD	METRIC (APPROX.)
⅛ teaspoon	0.5 mL
¼ teaspoon	1 mL
½ teaspoon	2 mL
¾ teaspoon	4 mL
1 teaspoon	5 mL
1 tablespoon	15 mL
¼ cup	59 mL
⅓ cup	79 mL
½ cup	118 mL
⅔ cup	156 mL
¾ cup	177 mL
1 cup	235 mL
2 cups or 1 pint	475 mL
3 cups	700 mL
4 cups or 1 quart	1 L

Weight Equivalents

US STANDARD	METRIC (APPROX.)
½ ounce	15 g
1 ounce	30 g
2 ounces	60 g
4 ounces	115 g
8 ounces	225 g
12 ounces	340 g
16 ounces or 1 pound	455 g

INDEX

Acknowledgments

I'd like to thank my daughter Claire, and the family and friends who have accepted that I have only one focus: food! They've also recognized that this obsession works to their advantage.

I'd also like to thank Hoss Zare and Gigi Abdalla, two fabulous chefs who have generously shared their culture through their cuisine.

Lastly, thanks to my editor, Anne Goldberg, and the Callisto Media staff.

About the Author

 **Dorothy Calimeris** is a food writer, blogger, and recipe developer. She is the author of five cookbooks, including *The Anti-Inflammatory Diet & Action Plan* and *The Good Life! Mediterranean Diet Cookbook*. She has a passion for creating recipes that use whole, real foods in ways that are quick, easily accessible, and don't sacrifice flavor. Visit her at DorothyEats.com.